TOP TRAILS (

NEVADA

INCLUDES GREAT BASIN NATIONAL PARK, VALLEY OF
FIRE AND CATHEDRAL GORGE STATE PARKS, AND
BASIN AND RANGE NATIONAL MONUMENT

by Eric Henze

Gone Beyond Guides
Publisher

Basin and Range National Monument

General Information

What is the Grand Circle?

So you've been done an Arizona vacation, maybe even Colorado and Utah, but have you done the Grand Circle? You may have heard of the term and likely know it well if you live within it. For those that don't know what the Grand Circle means, you aren't alone. It is, in a nutshell, one of the "must do" vacation destinations in North America.

The Grand Circle encompasses five southwestern states but more importantly, is so named because it contains the highest concentration of national and state parks in the United States. Within this 500-mile diameter area, there are almost 80 parks and hundreds of other attractions. Simply put, the Grand Circle is a bounty of fun and adventure. This isn't about going to Zion or the Grand Canyon, it's about going on a once in a lifetime vacation, something so incredible that it becomes one of the top things you have ever done.

Within the Grand Circle are attractions found nowhere else in the world. Some of these seem to defy the laws of physics while others defy the boundaries of what you thought was possible. I've taken folks into areas where nobody spoke a word because they simply had never seen land like this before. They were in speechless awe and it's true, the journey can be beyond words, the land can be that striking. Within it are timeless monoliths, thousands of arches, delicately balanced rocks, some of the wildest rapids in the world and the deepest canyons. It contains the darkest nighttime skies in North America and the brightest colors during the day. The land is a symphony, at times thunderous and deafening, at other times a single soft note trailing into the silence of a deep blue sky. Here there are hoodoos, goblins, fins, tall alpine peaks and slot canyon so narrow there is barely room for one person. There are red rock cliffs, sheer vertical walls of rock so high that they are the emotional equal in sandstone what Yosemite is in granite.

This is a place that resets a person. One can't help but slow to the pace of the land. A visit here is a mixture of relaxation and wonder. You will find yourself returning to the pace of nature as you venture farther from the pace of man. It brings with it a connectedness reminding the visitor the things that are truly important in life.

This is a land carved by water and wind over millions of years and the results are astounding natural works of art. It is no wonder that this area contains the largest concentration of national parks and national monuments in the United States. Sure, the circle contains the internationally known Grand Canyon and Zion, but these are just two of its twelve national parks. Add to this list another 30 national monuments, 3 national recreation areas, several tribal parks and 29 more state parks. Moreover, these are just the lands formally set aside.

By the numbers, most of the parks that make up the Grand Circle are within Utah and Arizona, but the full magnitude of the circle encompasses lands within Nevada, New Mexico, and Colorado as well. The imaginary circle is about 500 miles in diameter or roughly 126 million acres of land. As daunting as that sounds, one can comfortably visit 7-8 of the most popular national parks (and several other parks along the way) in 10 days. Of course, the more one is able to slow down and spend here, the more one will see, but the point is, if you are looking for a vacation where every day is different, you can experience a large and varied amount of places in a relatively short amount of time here.

Historically, the Grand Circle was a term created when the Southwest National Parks were just beginning. The NPS worked with the Union Pacific Railway

Parks Covered in This Book

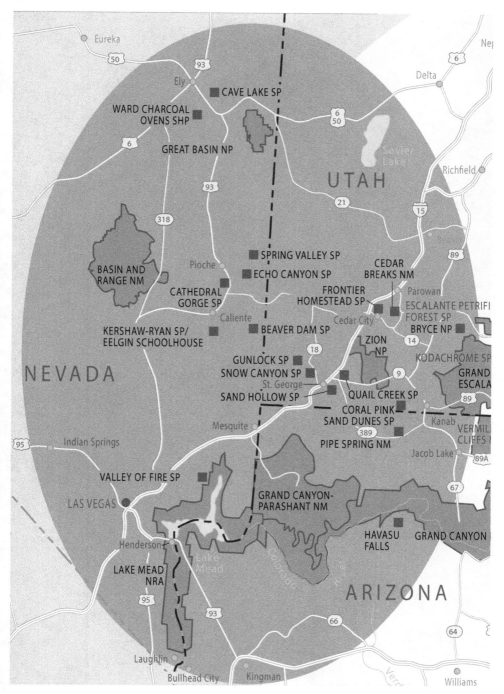

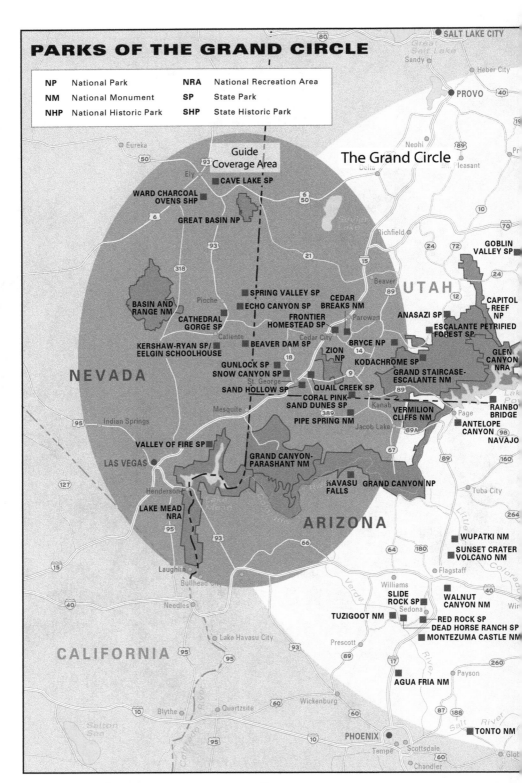

PARKS OF THE GRAND CIRCLE

NP	National Park	**NRA**	National Recreation Area
NM	National Monument	**SP**	State Park
NHP	National Historic Park	**SHP**	State Historic Park

Guide Coverage Area

The Grand Circle

SALT LAKE CITY
Great Salt Lake
Sandy
Heber City
PROVO
Nephi
Mt. Pleasant
Delta
Richfield
UTAH
Beaver

Eureka
Ely
CAVE LAKE SP
WARD CHARCOAL OVENS SHP
GREAT BASIN NP
GOBLIN VALLEY SP
CAPITOL REEF NP
SPRING VALLEY SP
CEDAR BREAKS NM
ANASAZI SP
ESCALANTE PETRIFIED FOREST SP
BASIN AND RANGE NM
Pioche
ECHO CANYON SP
CATHEDRAL GORGE SP
FRONTIER HOMESTEAD SP
Parowan
GLEN CANYON NRA
KERSHAW-RYAN SP/ EELGIN SCHOOLHOUSE
Caliente
BEAVER DAM SP
Cedar City
BRYCE NP
KODACHROME SP
GUNLOCK SP
ZION NP
GRAND STAIRCASE-ESCALANTE NM
NEVADA
SNOW CANYON SP
St. George
QUAIL CREEK SP
SAND HOLLOW SP
CORAL PINK SAND DUNES SP
Kanab
VERMILION CLIFFS NM
Page
RAINBOW BRIDGE
Mesquite
PIPE SPRING NM
Jacob Lake
ANTELOPE CANYON
NAVAJO
Indian Springs
VALLEY OF FIRE SP
GRAND CANYON-PARASHANT NM
LAS VEGAS
Henderson
HAVASU FALLS
GRAND CANYON NP
Tuba City
LAKE MEAD NRA
ARIZONA
WUPATKI NM
SUNSET CRATER VOLCANO NM
Laughlin
Bullhead City
Flagstaff
Needles
Williams
SLIDE ROCK SP
WALNUT CANYON NM
TUZIGOOT NM
Sedona
RED ROCK SP
DEAD HORSE RANCH SP
MONTEZUMA CASTLE NM
CALIFORNIA
Lake Havasu City
Prescott
AGUA FRIA NM
Payson
Blythe
Quartzsite
Wickenburg
Salton Sea
PHOENIX
TONTO NM
Tempe
Scottsdale
Chandler

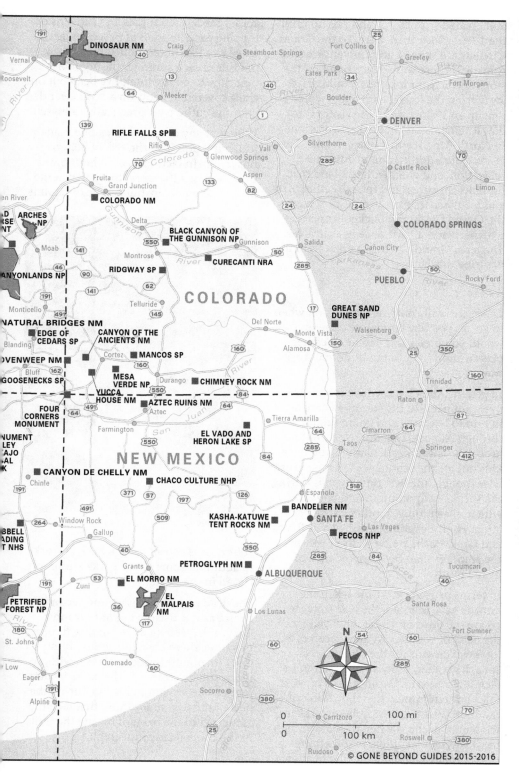

© GONE BEYOND GUIDES 2015-2016

and created trips by rail and bus up until the 1970's. Back then, a trip to the Grand Circle was a time of great adventure and romance. There were dance bands at the stops and as your tour bus would drive away from the lodge, employees would line up and "sing away" the visitors. Today, it remains one of the best vacations in North America that one can take. This is a vacation destination of adventure, relaxation, and wonder. It is a land that humbles, inspires, and refreshes the spirit and for those that know of it, they have the Grand Circle as a bucket list place to experience at least once in their lives. The term Grand Circle is a great term to describe this land.

When to Go

There are really only two factors on when to go, do you like temperate climates or would you prefer less people. Weather plays a hand in both but in different ways.

In general, the Grand Circle is a blisteringly hot place in the summer, starting in mid to late June and going full force through August. That doesn't seem to keep folks away, particularly if you have kids out for the school year. Temperature wise though, the best time to go is during the spring/early summer and fall/early winter. Elevation is another consideration. High elevation parks such as Bryce and Great Basin are typically cooler in the summer than say Canyonlands or Lake Powell.

In terms of going at a time when the crowds have thinned, the best times to go are the dead of winter, followed by the dead of summer. Winter receives a lot fewer crowds for the obvious reasons. It's colder, snowier, and wetter. In fact, it tends to be the antithesis of what folks have in mind when they think of the southwest. That said, these parks in winter are perhaps when they are at their most spectacular. There is something transformative about a dusting of snow

across the layered mesas and canyons or topping each hoodoo of Bryce. In fact, for places like Bryce, which receive tons of visitors each summer, the arguably best time to go is winter. I've been out on trails covered in snow on a crisp clear day with the entire park practically to myself.

Winter at any of the parks can be magical, but it does run the risk of being miserable. In fact, you could be snowed in, which isn't the worst thing that could happen to a person, but can be difficult if

Spires at Cathedral Gorge

your boss is expecting you back at work. In addition, some of the parks are simply closed in the winter.

The dead of summer is a good second choice as it is usually too hot for most. That said, given kids are out of school at this time, there are many whose lifestyles gives them nothing else to work with, so it can still be crowded. The parks in summer can be too hot to hike in during the heat of the day, so for those that take this tactic, get in the habit of hitting the trails in the cool of early morning.

Where to Go

If you think about it, there is a fair amount of irony in guidebooks that tell you the best places to go to avoid crowds. They are basically saying, we've learned all these secret cool places that no one goes to and we are now publishing this information in a globally available guidebook for anyone to read. If you see one of these sections, don't believe it, the word is already out on all these "secret places". In fact, places such as Havasu Falls are so impacted, it is nearly impossible to get a permit to hike the trail.

That said, there are some general tips to getting an otherwise crowded national park or monument to yourself. Take the Grand Canyon for example. This park receives some 4.5 million visitors to the South Rim alone. The vast majority of these folks don't hike any farther than to the overlooks. So simply getting out on any trail cuts the population of the park down by about 90%. If you've purchased this book, that means you like to hike, so you are on good footing right from the start.

There are other tips to share. In general, I've found that the more strenuous the hike is, the harder the trail is to get to, and the longer the trail's length, the greater the chances you will have the trail to yourself. If the trail is a short little paved walkway with interpretive signs, be prepared to share it. If it is one of the routes described in these guides, so rugged there isn't even a trail, be prepared to survive on your own because you are likely the only one out that way.

The same can be said about weather. Heat, rain, snow, and cold tend to filter out a fair amount of people. What's amazing about this is sometimes inclement weather will bring out the most unique views of a trail you will likely ever see. Now keep you in mind that you should add in a large degree of common sense. You don't want to have a slot canyon "all to yourself" in a thunderstorm or hike in the direct heat of a summer's day unless you are fully prepared and acclimated. Don't be stupid in your quest to have the place to yourself. The point here is, in general I've found a rather obvious truth. If a guidebook says it's secret, it isn't. The more remote a place is, the longer the hike, the steeper the inclines, the more extreme the journey, these all act as filters to minimizing the crowd factor.

Being Prepared

Hiking in the Grand Circle can be highly rewarding. However, don't let the desert fool you. This is an extreme environment, and one shouldn't just venture out without some forethought and preparation. This section seems straightforward, but as the rangers at the Grand Canyon can attest to, there are literally dozens of people that venture out into the wilderness with nothing more than enthusiasm. Since enthusiasm alone can really put a damper on your hike, here are some tips to make your hikes safer and more enjoyable.

Water

Rule of thumb; bring three quarts per person per day. Some folks prefer two 1.5-liter bottles; some find they can balance their day or backpacks out better with three 1.0-liter bottles. Make sure the bottles do not leak by turning them upside down to see if water comes out. If it's only a drip, it's still a problem.

Water is pretty heavy, but bringing more rather than less keeps you hydrated and allows you to go farther.

If you are traveling with small children, you will likely need to carry their water for them beyond one quart. Keep this in mind as you are packing.

Clothing

Bring layers as appropriate for the hike. This means if the temperatures are cooler when you are at rest; bring a layer or two to keep you warm. Windbreakers are great allies in keeping warmth in and cold out and are also lightweight. In really cold temps a good beanie helps as well as some 15% of your body temperature is lost through your head. If it looks like rain, bring a waterproof version of that windbreaker.

In the heat, most folks go with the t-shirt and shorts, which is fine, but definitely bring a hat. The heat can be oppressing, especially with no shade and that hat will definitely help. I also recommend a full brimmed hat over a baseball cap. This will provide more shade and definitely helps keep the back of your neck from getting sunburned.

In either hot or cold weather, bring another warm layer if you can. This is your emergency backup layer should you find yourself having to spend the night in the wilderness for whatever reason. A windbreaker that can be rolled up or a long sleeve shirt can make a big difference if you find yourself facing the setting sun with nothing but a t-shirt and shorts on a summer trip. I've also found it to be a good thing to have on hand for others that may need some warmth when you don't.

Boots, Tennis and Water Shoes

Most people will tend to go for their tennis shoes because they are comfortable and easier to lace up. That said, boots are preferred because they offer a lot more protection, especially around the ankles. Tennis shoes are great for flat surfaces, but boots are made for uneven terrain. It's like taking a sedan tire on a 4WD road instead of an all-terrain tire. You wouldn't do it to your car, don't do it to your feet. Where a good boot and also, be the boot. Wear it in before you start your hiking adventures so you don't get blisters.

If the trail involves some hiking in water, it really helps to have a pair of water shoes. They are lightweight and keep your boots dry. A dry boot makes for a happy hiker, whereas a wet boot can destroy your feet in short order.

Typical topography , Cave Lake State Park

Daypack

A decent no nonsense day back to hold everything is essential. At the end of the day, you just want something that will last a long time. The more parts the pack has, the more parts that can fail. Zipper quality is number one. Most otherwise solid daypacks fail because of the zipper.

Also, a little tip on the daypack. If you get one that zips like an upside down U, put the zippers on one side or the other, not at the top. I have seen and personally had a branch find its way between the two zippers at top and open the entire contents of the pack onto the trail. In my case, it opened on brushy 30-degree incline I was scrambling up and I watched my lunch and water roll downhill out of sight forever.

Other Gear

At this point, you have three quarts of water, a bunch of layers, some food, and no room for anything else right. Well, it can seem that way. What to bring is a balancing act. On the one hand, you want to be lightweight. The more stuff you have on your back, the more burdensome it will feel. On the other hand, you do want to be prepared. In the excellent book, Climbing Ice by Yvon Chouinard, he says something that is about as true a piece of advice I've ever heard in this context.

If you bring it, you will use it.

What this means is if you bring a sleeping bag, you will likely spend the night in it. If you bring rope, you will likely use that rope. So start with packing only what you need for the hike.

Essentials include:

- Water and some food
- A hat
- Extra clothing as appropriate
- Sunscreen

- A map and possibly this trail guide (if you feel you will need it to navigate the trail)

On top of this, I would seriously consider also bringing:

- Some form of fire, a lighter, or fire starter of some kind
- Compass
- Small first aid kit, a whistle, and reflector mirror (for emergencies)
- A sharp knife
- Moleskin (for blisters)
- Ibuprofen (to help if you aren't acclimated to the heat)
- Water purification tablets
- Small flashlight
- Cell phone
- GPS device

It's hard to come up with a list that works under all conditions and the above list is more geared towards summer hiking than winter, so adjust what you bring for cold, rain, or snow. Also, be sure to bring something fun, a little treat goes a long way and is much better appreciated on the trail. This falls under "being kind to yourself" which is described below.

Know Yourself

Gung Ho-ness

Many of these trails are steep and long. Add in that you are at high elevations and the temperatures are hot means many of the hikes in this book can be challenging. With that in mind, choose a hike that is appropriate for you. You will enjoy the hike more and plus; you will be able to go on another hike the next day. Know your physical limitations and don't test them to the point that you will need to be rescued.

Thunderstorm in the Basin and Range

Find your pace

Great hiking partners are not only experienced; they are great for each other because they both travel at the same pace. Start by finding your own pace and ask others to share that pace with you. If you are the faster traveler, slow down to the pace of the other person or group.

Take Breaks, Eat Snacks

Taking a ten-minute break every hour actually improves your stamina, allowing you to enjoy the hike more and go longer. Resting helps remove metabolic waste products such as lactic acid and gives your body time to flush them out. Eating snacks and drinking fluids helps refuel your body so you can continue onwards happy and content.

Time Flies

Being stuck on the trail after the sun sets isn't much fun, well unless there's a full moon out and no canopy to block the light. That can actually be a lot of fun and is highly recommended. Wait, the point I'm trying to make here is if you are out in the wilderness, watch your time and be aware of how long it took you to get to your turn around point. If the trail starts as a major descent, some of the steeper trails require twice as much time for returning up then it took getting down. The Grand Canyon is a good example of this. Being stuck in areas where the temperature drops dramatically at night is also a concern. Here, the The Narrows hike in Zion is a great example. Also, if you think you might be caught out in the dark, having a little flashlight, per person, can be a lifesaver.

Don't be afraid to abort the trip

If you or another hiker is showing signs of exhaustion, heat stroke, hypothermia or if the weather doesn't look like its adding up right, don't hesitate to turn back. Typically, these trips are planned far in advance and there is plenty of anticipation and excitement, but nothing is worth serious health issues or worse from not making the right decision. If someone doesn't feel they are up to a hike or someone in the group feels they may be putting themselves in danger, take their concerns seriously. Heat stroke and hypothermia can get serious and can lead to death.

Hypothermia, altitude sickness, and heat exhaustion have nothing to do with physical ability. I've seen firsthand the symptoms of each of these health issues and everyone that experienced them started out in terrific shape. It can hit hard and quickly. The typical "first signs" that I've seen are loss of mental sharpness and generally just out of it. The victim appears drunk and off, but otherwise may seem "themselves" at times. Don't second-guess here, if your buddy isn't acting like his or her normal self; stop, assess and remediate the issue. Don't keep pressing on.

The Hazardous H's + Altitude Sickness

The below is put out by the National Park Service and gives a good overview of some of the health issues to look out for while hiking. Since some of the trails within the Grand Circle are at altitude, a description of altitude sickness or acute mountain sickness (AMS) is also included.

Heat Exhaustion

The result of dehydration due to intense sweating. Hikers can lose one or two quarts (liters) of water per hour.

Symptoms: pale face, nausea, vomiting, cool and moist skin, headache, cramps.

Treatment: drink water with electrolytes, eat high-energy foods (with fats and sugars), rest in the shade for 30-45 minutes, and cool the body by getting wet.

Heatstroke

A life-threatening emergency where the body's heat regulating mechanisms become overwhelmed by a combination of internal heat production and environmental demands. Your body loses its ability to cool itself. Grand Canyon has two to three cases of heatstroke a year. Untreated heat exhaustion can lead to heatstroke.

Symptoms: flushed face, dry skin, weak and rapid pulse, high core body temperature, confusion, poor judgment or inability to cope, unconsciousness, seizures.

Treatment: the heatstroke victim must be cooled immediately! Continuously pour water on the victim's head and torso, fan to create an evaporative cooling effect. Immerse the victim in cold water if possible. Move the victim to shade and remove excess clothing. The victim needs evacuation to a hospital. Someone should go for help while attempts to cool the victim continue.

Hyponatremia (water intoxication)

An illness that mimics the early symptoms of heat exhaustion. It is the result of low sodium in the blood caused by drinking too much water and losing too much salt through sweating.

Symptoms: nausea, vomiting, altered mental states, confusion, frequent urination. The victim may appear intoxicated. In extreme cases seizures may occur.

Treatment: have the victim eat salty foods, slowly drink sports drinks with electrolytes, and rest in the shade. If mental alertness decreases, seek immediate help!

Hypothermia

A life-threatening emergency where the body cannot keep itself warm, due to exhaustion and exposure to cold, wet, windy weather.

Symptoms: uncontrolled shivering, poor muscle control, careless attitude. Look for signs of the "umbles" - stumbling, mumbling, fumbling, grumbling.

Treatment: remove wet clothing and put on dry clothing, drink warm sugary liquids, warm victim by body contact with another person, protect from wind, rain, and cold.

Altitude Sickness

Altitude sickness is your body not being able to acclimate to altitude. If untreated, it can lead to high altitude pulmonary oedema (HAPE) which is a life threatening condition where your lungs fill with fluid, making it difficult to breath. It can also lead to high altitude cerebral oedema (HACE), which is a buildup of fluid in your brain. Both can cause death within hours if not treated.

Symptoms: The most common symptom is typically a headache similar to that felt with a hangover. Some folks will feel nausea and may vomit as well as a general malaise feeling, and dizziness.

Treatment: If you are experiencing AMS, the best and only treatment is descending. Altitude sickness is not uncommon, especially if you have ascended in elevation too fast, starting at elevations of 8200 feet (2500 m). While it is common, some people are only slightly affected,

while others feel so bad they have to turn around. For all, even those slightly affected, be self-aware as it can lead to pulmonary and cerebral oedema, which are very serious conditions.

If You Get Lost

Daniel Boone once said, "I have never been lost, but I will admit to being confused for several weeks." If you do get lost, you will quickly realize you aren't Daniel Boone and wished you had of paid more attention to all those nifty tricks you might have seen on those survival shows. Never fear, this book might just save you. Read the following tips if you happen to get lost.

- Stay calm. The sun's setting and you still haven't found the trail, let alone your car. This is not a time to freak out. Take some deep breaths and stay calm. You will get through this. I realize if you are freaking out, reading this won't help one bit. I recommend rereading the first sentence in this bullet point until it makes sense. Once you are thinking rationally, continue to the next bullet.

- Ration water and food. Stay hungry, ration your water, don't eat and drink everything at once.

- Readjust your schedule to maximize for hydration. Water loss has now become your biggest enemy. This means hiking during the cool of the morning and evening, while hunkering down at mid-day. Aim for shade and stay put during the heat of the day. Remember, the power of threes when it comes to survival. Though you will be incredibly hungry, you can survive three weeks without food. For wa-

Wheeler Peak in Great Basin National Park

ter, that time period is only three days (and for air, three minutes). Water loss is the biggest barrier to you surviving or not if you are lost in the desert.

- Make a plan. If you have a compass, see a landmark, can get a sense of direction from the sun, use all these things to help make a plan of action. This starts by staying calm. With calmness, you can think. In thought, you can assess what you know (and what you don't know). From this catalog of observations, you can make a plan. Try to remain rational and fact based in your observations, its okay to make an assumption, but assess how confident you are of these assumptions.

- Stay at an even calm pace, pick your path. Look ahead to where you want to go, aim for paths of least resistance and effort versus paths that are harder to get through, if possible. Don't rush your walking, stay calm.

- Follow a road, a trail, or a route. If you see a road or a trail, take it. You have greatly increased your chances of being found or finding a way out yourself.

- Stay off the ground during the day. Finding shade is important when resting as the ground temperature can by 30 degrees hotter than the air temperature.

- Hike together at the pace of the slowest member and only separate if someone is injured.

- Stay with your car. If you are near your car, stay with it. It will make finding you easier and will provide shade, shelter and hopefully some food.

Eastern Nevada

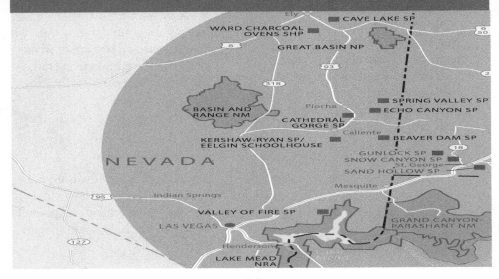

Valley of Fire State Park

Quick Facts

Official Park Website:

- http://parks.nv.gov/parks/valley-of-fire-state-park/

Visitor Center:

- (702) 397-2088

Park Accessibility:

- Okay for 2WD and RVs
- Day and Overnight Use

Experience Level:

- Family Friendly to Casual Hiker

Camping in Park:

There are 2 campgrounds in the park plus 3 group sites.

- Combined total of 72 T/RV, drinking water, restrooms, showers, dump station, power and water hookups, first come-first served, contact visitor center to reserve group sites

Lodging and Dining in Park:

- None

Nearest Town with Amenities:

- Echo Bay Resort and Marina on Lake Mead is 21 mi / 34 km from park.

Getting There:

- From Las Vegas, NV: Take I-15 North to Valley of Fire Highway. Total distance is 52 mi / 84 km to park.

Valley of Fire State Park

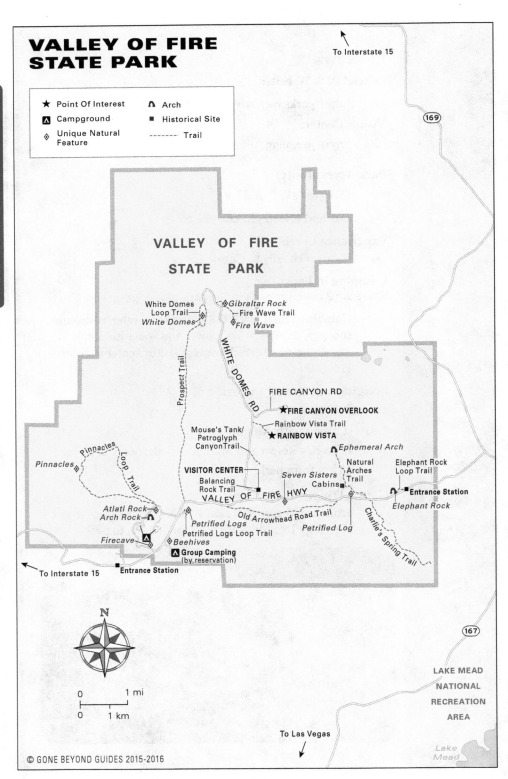

VALLEY OF FIRE STATE PARK

Valley of Fire

Legend
- ★ Point Of Interest
- △ Campground
- ◇ Unique Natural Feature
- ∩ Arch
- ■ Historical Site
- ------- Trail

To Interstate 15

169

VALLEY OF FIRE STATE PARK

White Domes Loop Trail
White Domes
◇ Gibraltar Rock
Fire Wave Trail
Fire Wave

Prospect Trail

WHITE DOMES RD

FIRE CANYON RD
★ FIRE CANYON OVERLOOK

Rainbow Vista Trail
★ RAINBOW VISTA

Mouse's Tank/ Petroglyph Canyon Trail

∩ Ephemeral Arch

Pinnacles
Pinnacles Loop Trail

VISITOR CENTER
Balancing Rock Trail
Seven Sisters
Cabins
Natural Arches Trail

Elephant Rock Loop Trail

VALLEY OF FIRE HWY
∩ ■ Entrance Station
Elephant Rock

Atlatl Rock
Arch Rock ∩
Old Arrowhead Road Trail

Firecave
△
Petrified Logs
Petrified Logs Loop Trail
Petrified Log

◇ Beehives

Charlie's Spring Trail

△ Group Camping (by reservation)

To Interstate 15
■ Entrance Station

N

0 ——— 1 mi
0 ——— 1 km

167

LAKE MEAD NATIONAL RECREATION AREA

To Las Vegas

Lake Mead

What Makes Valley of Fire State Park Special

- Nevada's oldest and largest state park and one of the best park names ever!

- Breathtaking scenery of red sandstone features, all varied and unique

- Close to Las Vegas, makes a great side trip to refresh from the excesses of The Strip

What a park! If you are one of the many coming from California for a jaunt into Las Vegas, you have likely flown over Valley of Fire SP as you make your final descent. It's the beacon of intriguing red sandstone that stands out amongst the dry landscape of the Mojave Desert just before landing. If you can pry yourself away from the gaming tables, this park won't disappoint. Arches, slot canyons, petrified wood and candy caned striped rock formations greet the visitor. It's a no brainer as to why this was Nevada's first state park, because it is one of the coolest places in the Southwest.

Hiking Valley of Fire State Park

Old Arrowhead Road
Moderate to Strenuous – (6.8 mi / 10.9 km), round trip, allow 1 hour

The Old Arrowhead Road follows the remains of the first all-weather road connecting Salt Lake City to Los Angeles, by way of Las Vegas. There is a little historical marker dedicated to this "milestone of progress". The Arrowhead Road started in 1914 and began receiving motorists in 1915. This was a novel time for the automobile; roads were being built as fast as trains were declining as the means to get around the country. It was a time when the personal freedom of being able

to "hit the road" and go anywhere your car could take you was a new thought. By 1924, Highways 91 and Interstate 15 took over as the main routes. This hike encompasses some beautiful scenery. Most walk the short extension near Elephant Rock and leave the longer trail for folks who can drop one car at one end and shuttle back to the other.

Petrified Logs Loop
Easy – (0.3 mi / 0.5 km), round trip, allow 15 to 30 minutes

This short interpretative trail is described for one reason; petrified logs are downright awesome. Simply put, this area was once part of a super continent called Pangea that sat near the equator. Mind you, this was 225 million years ago, but still, nothing puts context that there used to be an ancient pine forest here than a testimony of petrified logs. There are two locations where the logs can be viewed and interpretative signs along the way.

Pinnacles Loop
Moderate to Strenuous – (4.5 mi / 7.2 km), round trip, allow 1 hour

This is great remote hike, with possibilities of seeing no other hiker. From the trailhead near the Atlatl Rock parking area, head up the main wash, following marked signs. You'll enter into an area of sharp pinnacles, with tons of exploration possibilities. There is some scrambling and the trail does get faint in areas as you make your way through the pinnacles and back down an alluvial fan to the parking lot.

Prospect Trail
Moderate to Strenuous – (4.6 mi / 7.4 km), one way, allow 2-3 hours

The Prospect Trail is another there and back trail with one end starting at the White Domes parking area and the other end at Highway 169 near the Petrified Logs area. This trail is best done with

The remarkable colors of Valley of Fire State Park

two cars and is easier, (downhill), if you start from the White Domes parking lot. Prospect Trail gives a sense of deep immersion into the park's wilderness and is one of the best hikes for feeling remote and "away from it all". It starts by following nearly half of the White Dome Trail before continuing south at the White Dome/Prospect Trail fork. From here, the trail continues to navigate through cross channels and small canyons. There is some scrambling at a few stretches along this part, but nothing major. For the last stretch, the trail empties into an alluvial fan that is crossed to connect to the Valley of Fire Highway 169.

Balancing Rock

Easy – (0.1 mi / 0.2 km), round trip, allow 15 minutes

If you make a stop at the visitor center, be sure to take this short trail to a large precariously tilted square shaped rock that looks as if at any moment it will fall over, crushing any and all in its path. Great photo op!

Mouse's Tank

Easy – (1.4 mi / 2.3 km), round trip, allow 30 minutes

Mouse's Tank and Atlatl Rock together hold some of the largest concentrations of petroglyphs in Nevada, comprising of historical markings by different culture groups, with some being 3,000 years old.

The trail is quite sandy and typically very busy. Either try to go at sun up or just as the sun is setting to minimize crowds. Petroglyphs tend to be more noticeable in indirect light and with a fair amount of patience. It is easy to miss the less obvious ones. Pay particular attention to the north face of canyon walls, there are literally thousands of various symbols and artistic figures. Some are closer to eye level, while others are high up on cliff faces, as if as a test of bravery.

The trail ends at a natural round stone tank that holds water year round in all but the driest of years. It is named after a Southern Paiute Indian named "Little Mouse", who used this location to hide out in the 1890's. Little Mouse was known for thievery and general local nuisance, going on occasional drunken bouts of craziness. He hid out in the area because he was accused of murdering two prospectors. Whether he actually did or not is not actually known, though it is known he was surrounded a few miles away and in refusing to give up, was shot and killed.

Rainbow Vista

Moderate – (2.1 mi / 3.4 km), round trip, allow 1-2 hours

Most take this hike to get a great view of Fire Canyon from the overlook at the end of this there and back trail. This trail offers full immersion up a small canyon, with stunning rock formations along the way. The trailhead itself is a great pull off spot to take pictures of the landscape to the north, which can be quite inviting under mixed lighting conditions, especially in the spring after a storm. The one downside to this trail is that for the most part, the trail floor is deep sand, making the going a bit harder. Once inside the canyon and towards the end point at Fire Canyon overlook, there are caves and other nooks and crannies to explore.

White Domes Loop

Moderate – (1.0 mi / 1.6 km), round trip, allow 45 minutes to 1 hour

The White Domes Loop showcases the diversity of the park's contrasting rock, with just about every color in the sandstone palate. There is a bit of minor rock scrambling involved that leads to a little slot canyon. The slot canyon is just 0.25 miles long, but is pleasantly narrow. As you make your way back on the loop, look for an arch.

The one other aspect of this trail is the ruin of a stone building, which was used in the 1966 movie, "The Professionals", staring Lee Marvin and Burt Lancaster. The movie was about a kidnapped wife of a Texas millionaire, who hires four rough and tumble characters to get her back. It was nominated for three Academy Awards.

Fire Wave Trail

Moderate to Strenuous – (1.3 mi / 2.1 km), round trip, allow 1 hour

This hike is certainly one of the top picks in terms of great hikes. It's the unique sandstone formations that really make this hike outstanding, which is saying something, as there are many unique rock formations in Valley of Fire SP. The highlights of the hike are swirls of red and white rock layers that have then been eroded into graceful curves of slickrock. The formations here defy the imagination and are a photographers dream. While the hike itself can be done in an hour or less, give yourself more time to take in the vividly crisp colors of rock as natural art.

Natural Arches

Moderate – (5.0 mi / 8.0 km), round trip, allow 2 to 4 hours

The first thing to know about this trail is that the main attraction, a natural arch that looked like a dragon feeding it's young, collapsed in 2010. It fell from natural causes and no one was hurt. Now just the broken remnants remain. The good news is the views on this hike are stunning in their own right. The trail is on the trail map but isn't given much attention in the brochure covering the main hikes, making Natural Arches a great hike to get away from it all, even during crowded weekends.

The trail follows a sandy wash of pink and white canyon sand, deep enough in spots to test the hiker. Heading up canyon, the wash narrows after about a mile with a few short scrambles. This portion is not well marked, but is obvious enough, despite a couple of side canyons that quickly become dead ends if you should take a wrong turn. The trail gives the hiker ample views of this amazing landscape, and while the showcase dragon arch is gone, there are a few arches to be seen that are cool in their own right.

A nice place to hang out

There is a humongous balancing rock 2.4 miles that makes for a pleasant stop before heading back.

Elephant Rock Loop

Easy – (1.2 mi / 1.9 km), round trip, allow 30 minutes

This is a super family friendly trail that is fairly flat and easy to navigate for all ages. It is 0.4 miles round trip if you just want to see the Elephant Rock or 1.2 miles for the whole loop. The rock is just off the main highway, however there is no parking here, so head first to the East Entrance parking lot. From there, hike from the self-pay station and about 0.1 miles into the trail take a left to lead you right on up to Elephant Rock. The loop continues parallel to the road before bearing right and looping back around past some interesting rock formations.

Charlie's Spring Trail

Moderate to Strenuous – (6.7 mi / 10.8 km), round trip, allow 3-4 hours

This trail is seldom traveled and leads to a nice watery oasis fed by an underground spring. You will see tamarisk and cattails downstream of the spring before the water is reclaimed by the earth. For the most part, the trail follows an obvious wash, with one small dry waterfall and an equally small slot canyon before the reveal of the watery oasis. One half mile into the trail is a large memorial for John Clark, an honorably discharged Sergeant who died in route to Salt Lake City in 1915, presumably from thirst.

The journey to the spring is 2.75 miles. From here, you can either turn around or continue up the wash and bushwhack your way back. To do the latter, continue up the wash until you reach a power line road on your right coming into the wash. Take this road and continue until you see the road cross on your left and follow it up a hill and over to the next wash north of you. Continue on this wash in a north-westerly direction looking for a large solitary sandstone monolith as a marker. Once you see this outcrop, head towards it back to the highway. Head left on the Valley of Fire Highway back to your car.

Quick Facts

Official Park Website:

- http://www.nps.gov/lake

Visitor Center:

- (702) 293-8990

Park Accessibility:

- Okay for 2WD and RVs
- Day and Overnight Use

Experience Level:

- Family Friendly – Experienced Hiker

Camping in Park:

- There are numerous campgrounds in the park, information can be found here: http://www.nps.gov/lake/planyourvisit/campgrounds.htm

Lodging in Park:

- There is a multitude of lodging options within the park, details can be found here: http://www.nps.gov/lake/planyourvisit/lodging.htm

Dining in Park:

- Lots of dining opportunities, details here: http://www.nps.gov/lake/planyourvisit/wheretoeat.htm

Nearest Town with Amenities:

- There are multiple areas within the park that offer full amenities, including Echo Bay. Outside the park, Boulder City, NV is close to the southwest section of the park

Getting There:

- From Las Vegas, NV: take I-515 South to US-93 South 26 mi / 42 km to the southwestern park entrance

Lake Mead National Recreation Area

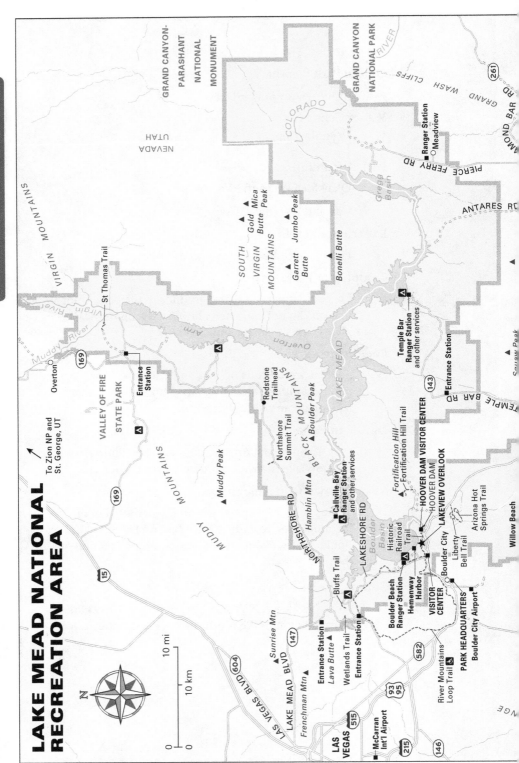

Lake Mead

EASTERN NEVADA

LAKE MEAD NATIONAL RECREATION AREA

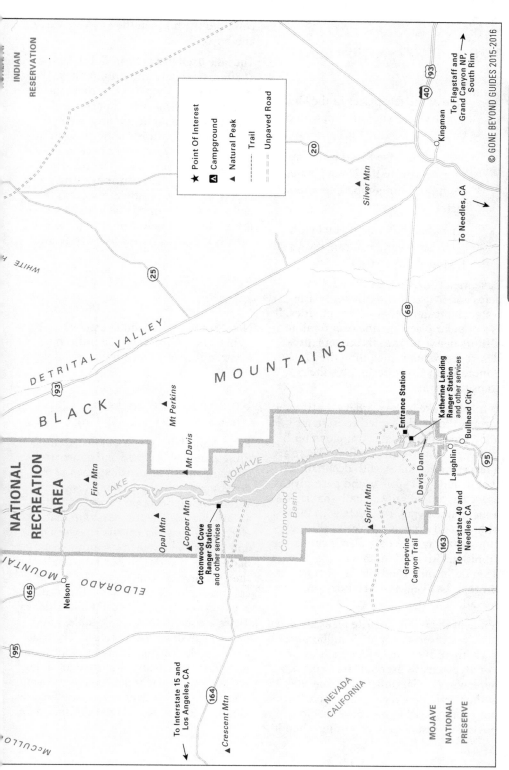

Lake Mead

Map Legend

★ Point Of Interest
△ Campground
▲ Natural Peak
----- Trail
==== Unpaved Road

© GONE BEYOND GUIDES 2015-2016

INDIAN RESERVATION

WHITE H

WHITE H

93
25
20
68
93
40
95
165
95
164

DETRITAL VALLEY

BLACK MOUNTAINS

NATIONAL RECREATION AREA

ELDORADO MOUNTAIN

Nelson

▲ Fire Mtn
▲ Opal Mtn
▲ Copper Mtn
▲ Crescent Mtn
▲ Mt Davis
▲ Mt Perkins
▲ Silver Mtn
▲ Spirit Mtn

LAKE

MOHAVE

Cottonwood Basin

■ Cottonwood Cove Ranger Station
and other services

■ Entrance Station

Katherine Landing Ranger Station
and other services

Bullhead City

Davis Dam

Laughlin

Kingman

Grapevine Canyon Trail

McCULLO

To Interstate 15 and
Los Angeles, CA

To Interstate 40 and
Needles, CA

To Needles, CA

To Flagstaff and
Grand Canyon NP,
South Rim

NEVADA
CALIFORNIA

MOJAVE NATIONAL PRESERVE

What Makes Lake Mead National Recreation Area Special

- One of the few places in the Grand Circle where you can rent a house boat
- When full, Lake Mead is the largest reservoir in the United States, serving 20 million people across 3 states
- Knowing that even if you lose it all in Las Vegas, you can always go hiking at Lake Mead

Lake Mead NRA covers over 1.3 million acres and is used primarily for boating, water skiing and other water activities. It is a popular place, getting over 6 million visitors per year. The land covers three desert ecosystems, including the Mojave, Sonoran and Great Basin, plus their transition zones.

While the lake is the primary destination for most folks, the varied ecosystems allows for hiking that is unique in both scenery and surrounding flora. There are a few standout hikes, with destinations that include hot springs and petroglyphs as well as an old railway path that is now a maintained trail, complete with the old railroad tunnels one walks through along the way. The park also includes the ambitious River Mountains Loop Trail, a 35-mile "mini Grand Circle", that passes through Las Vegas and Henderson, Nevada.

Some of the NPS's favorite picks are listed here, but given this is a 1.3-million-acre park, there are many other trails as well. For an extensive list of all area hikes go here: www.birdandhike.com. The site's author, PhD Ecologist, Jim Boone, has put a lot of passion into his effort to document just about everything when it comes to the hikes in the Las Vegas area and beyond.

The lake itself hasn't been full since the 1980's, as demand and drought have taken a toll on supply. As of 2010, the lake was at a bleak 39% capacity and fears that it would be too low to run the hydroelectric facilities come closer to reality with each year. As far back as 2002, boat launches have had to be relocated or have been closed altogether. This story is playing out currently throughout the entire western United States and all who live under the shadow of drought look each winter for a return to more average rainfall levels.

Hiking in Lake Mead National Recreation Area

Note: Some of these hikes can be extremely hot in the summer and can be hazardous to one's health due to dehydration and heat stroke.

River Mountains Loop Trail
Strenuous – (35.0 mi / 56.3 km), one-way

River Mountains is the Cadillac of trails. Professionally designed and constructed, covering multiple jurisdictions, the trail does a great job of providing residents with recreational opportunities within an urban area. The trail is a loop that effectively "starts" near the Hoover Dam and heads clockwise first south to Boulder City, NV and then north through the outskirts of Henderson, NV before connecting back to the dam. The trail is paved and great for a solid bike ride. There are restrooms, picnic tables and even an air stand for bicyclists. The trail can be picked up at a number of locations including the Historic Railroad Trail described below. The trail even has its own website: http://rivermountainstrail.org/. Go there for maps and full description.

Historic Railroad Trail

Moderate – (4.4 mi / 7.1 km), round trip, allow 3 – 4 hours

This is a fun hike that follows along an old railroad track from Hoover Dam. The railway was once used to haul the massive turbines and at five points of construction, the railroad carved tunnels through solid rock. The tunnels are 25 feet high. The easygoing wide dirt path allows for a pleasant stroll, with views of Lake Mead in the near distance.

Historic Railroad Trail

Arizona Hot Spring

Moderate – (6.5 mi / 10.5 km), round trip, allow 5 hours, including soak time

Within Lake Mead NRA is an area of minor active volcanism. While it may be awhile before one will have to dodge a lava flow, it is possible to warm one's bones in a natural hot spring. The majority of the hike is through a volcanic slot canyon, providing a different geological context from the usual sandstone slick rock.

Take the Hot Springs Canyon Route, starting in a clockwise direction from

the trailhead. One can choose either the lower or the upper route. While the lower route does contain a class three scramble up a rock wall, there are some good handholds allowing most to navigate this dryfall. If climbing rocks isn't your thing, the upper route bypasses the scramble but is a bit longer.

As you draw up the route, the canyon becomes much narrower and you will need to walk in the stream itself. The warmth of the water is evident from the start. It's best to wear hiking boots that you can get wet, as the rock is a bit rough. There is a sturdy 20-foot ladder to climb at the end just before the hot springs.

The hot springs run at an average temperature of 111 degrees. The water is clear and inviting, though it is advised on the trail not to ingest the water or get it up your nose due to amoebas that are native to the hot springs. The amoeba, Naegleria fowleri, is rare, but lethal. Over the course of 9 years, from 2002 to 2011, the Center of Disease Control noted just 33 cases nationwide, but with a 98% death rate. With those statistics, odds of being affected by this amoeba are rare, but if you do, the only upside is you will finally get around to creating a will and choosing a cool epitaph. All in all, just don't ingest the water, either consciously or accidentally through the nose.

Once you've had a nice soak, continue clockwise; now onto White Rock Canyon Route for more stunning volcanic scenery as you walk back to your car. Note that it's common to see various items that were forgotten at the spring, don't forget your stuff before you leave.

Bluffs Trail

Moderate – (1.8 mi / 2.9 km), round trip, allow 1 hour

Bluff's Trail is there and back hike up a dry desert ridge to a minor summit. There are views of Lake Mead and the surrounding territory from the top.

Grapevine Canyon Trail
Moderate – (3.0 mi / 4.8 km), round trip, allow 1 – 2 hours

This is a pleasant hike with a small stream and other water features, as well as some unusual sandstone features along the way. The trail lands at a series of well-defined and easily found petroglyphs at a quarter mile in. There is a small but lush desert oasis further upstream with a waterfall at 1.5 miles.

Northshore Summit Trail
Easy – (0.6 mi / 1.0 km), round trip, allow 30 minutes

While this does have about 200 feet in elevation gain, the short distance makes this an easy hike to see some of the desert surrounding Lake Mead. No view of the lake itself, but the scenery is spectacular. The trail does have two routes to the top, allowing for a loop hike.

Redstone Trail
Easy – (0.5 mi / 0.8 km), round trip, allow 30 minutes

Near the Redstone Picnic area is an eroded layer of red sandstone that can be explored. This is a nice easy stroll and the tilted layers of sandstone are worth seeing up close. Plenty of opportunities to scramble up red rock islands. The picnic area has a lot of nice scenery as well. Great place for a lunch and hike during the cooler months.

St. Thomas Trail
Easy – (3.0 mi / 4.8 km), round trip, allow 90 minutes

One of the upsides to a drought is the re-surfacing of St. Thomas, a Mormon ghost town. The town was created in 1865 and had a population of 274 residents in 1930 before the townsfolk were asked to relocate. The small agricultural community moved to Logandale-Overton. Though most of the ghost town is made up of foundation structures only, it's still easy to piece together the layout of the settlement. Pick up a brochure from the ranger station to guide you. If you are looking for a scary hike, this is a good pick. Even in the daytime, many find it to be a spooky experience.

Redstone

Wetlands Trail

Easy – (1.3 mi / 2.1 km), round trip, allow 30 minutes

A short loop trail to Las Vegas Wash, a Lake Mead tributary. The trail travels within a riparian ecosystem along the water's edges, which is in contrast to the dry surroundings. Opportunity for wildlife viewing and late afternoon photo opportunities.

Liberty Bell Arch

Strenuous – (2.8 mi / 4.5 km), round trip, allow 2 hours

Liberty Bell Arch Trail is in the same vicinity as the Arizona Hot Spring Trail but is vastly different. The trail is exposed for nearly the entire length, providing some unique features on the way up to an overlook. This is typically a hot and dry dusty hike, so hot that the NPS has closed it to hiking during the summer months. There are two highlights beyond the views, a misshapen arch whose silhouette at the proper angle looks like the Liberty Bell and an old mine, complete with a dangerous, but inviting shaft and slowly decaying equipment. At the top, the views are commanding in every direction.

Fortification Hill

Strenuous – (4.0 mi / 6.4 km), round trip, allow 2 - 3 hours

This is a strenuous but otherwise straightforward there and back hike up to the top of Fortification Hill. Via the Ridge Route, the trail starts out climbing a sandy ridge, taking the hiker to a class 3 scramble up a rocky hill. From there, the trail dog legs to the left for the final approach to the summit. Along with the great views of Lake Mead, there is a summit register and marker. If bagging a peak is on your bucket list, this is an easy way to mark it off and get some good scenery along the way.

Lake Mead Muddy Mountains Wilderness

Beaver Dam State Park

Quick Facts

Official Park Website:

- http://parks.nv.gov/parks/beaver-dam-state-park/

Visitor Center:

- None in park, contact (775) 728-4460

Park Accessibility:

- Okay for 2WD and RVs
- Day and Overnight Use

Experience Level:

- Family Friendly to Casual Hiker

Camping in Park:

- Campground A and B: Total of 33 T/RV sites, drinking water in season, vault toilets, no hookups, first come-first served

Lodging and Dining in Park:

- None

Nearest Town with Amenities:

- Panaca, NV is 37 mi / 60 km from park

Getting There:

- From St George, UT: Take UT-18 North to UT-219 West to FR 001/White Rocks Road and then to FR 017/Enterprise Road. Total distance is 71 mi / 114 km to park.

Beaver Dam State Park

What Makes Beaver Dam Special

- Remote hiking opportunities within pinyon juniper forest of the high desert of Nevada

- Actual beavers, though mainly you'll see more beaver dams and other evidence

- Nice long canyon views and riparian hikes

Beaver Dam State Park is about a three-hour drive from Las Vegas and it is quite different from the city that never sleeps. The park has gentle streams, inviting waterfalls and deep canyons to explore in a setting of lush ponderosa pine and riparian flora.

Hiking Beaver Dam State Park

Waterfall Trail
Easy – (2.4 mi / 3.9 km), round trip, allow 30 minutes

This is another there and back trail as well as the first trail built back in the 1930's by the Civilian Conservation Corp. The trail ambles up Sheep Canyon through volcanic rock and willow trees to a small waterfall and pool. Further up is a hot spring that is cool to visit but not recommended for use due to health risks from the water.

Beaver Dam Wash Trail
Easy – (4.4 mi / 7.1 km), round trip, allow 30 minutes

This is the longest trail in the park and for the most part follows along Beaver Dam Wash as the trail name suggests. The trail travels through a diverse ecosystem as you walk alongside a small creek. The area has seen some flooding and the trail has been washed out down near the creek making it hard to follow.

Oak Knoll Trail
Easy – (0.6 mi / 1.0 km), round trip, allow 30 minutes

This easy hike takes you down to the Headwaters and Pine Creeks and is a favorite of anglers. The decent fishing aside, the area is a great place to enjoy not one but two mountain streams.

Interpretative Trail
Moderate – (1.6 mi / 2.6 km), round trip, allow 30 minutes

The short half mile Interpretative Trail climbs steadily to a view of the confluence of the two park streams, the canyon below, and the Hamblin ranch site, an early settler to the area. There are also examples of volcanic hoodoos that can be seen.

Kershaw - Ryan State Park

Quick Facts

Official Park Website:

- http://parks.nv.gov/parks/kershaw-ryan-state-park/

Visitor Center:

- None in park, contact (775) 726-3564

Park Accessibility:

- Okay for 2WD and RVs
- Day and Overnight Use

Experience Level:

- Family Friendly to Casual Hiker

Camping in Park:

- Kershaw-Ryan Campground: 15 T/RV, drinking water, restrooms, showers, dumping station, no hookups, shade ramadas at each site, first come-first served

Lodging and Dining in Park:

- None

Nearest Town with Amenities:

- Caliente, NV is 4 mi / 6 km from park.

Getting There:

- From St George, UT: Take UT-18 North to UT-56 West to NV-319 West to US-93 South to Road 55/ Kershaw Park Entrance Road. Total distance is 114 mi / 183 km to park.

Park Entrance

What Makes Kershaw-Ryan State Park Special

Once a homestead that grew fruit trees and grape vines in a remote section of desert

It is now a park that protects this oasis of spring fed water surrounded by rugged countryside

The first settlers, Sam and Hannah Kershaw, must have smiled ear to ear on finding this place. Tucked away in a little side canyon at the northern end of Rainbow Canyon was exactly what a pioneer family needed. Here they found an area surrounded by towering canyon walls up to 700 feet high, which protected them, and a wonderful spring fed pond that gave them life. Folks prospered here making use of the abundant water to grow crops and fruit orchards.

Today the park maintains the peaceful oasis portion of what the early settlers experienced along with camping, picnicking and a couple of hiking opportunities. The park itself is quaint and tranquil. There's even a small wading pool to cool off in after the hike is done. The trails that surround the homestead are rugged and dry high desert, offering outstanding views. The Union Pacific Railroad can be heard regularly echoing through the canyon.

Hiking Kershaw-Ryan State Park

Rattlesnake Canyon Trail
Easy – (1.0 mi / 1.6 km), round trip, allow 15 minutes

Short loop trail into Rattlesnake Canyon giving great views into the park and the surrounding canyon. Connect with this trail via the parking lot.

Canyon Overlook Loop
Moderate – (1.4 mi / 2.3 km), round trip, allow 45 minutes to 1 hour

The longest hike in the park. This trail climbs up higher and deeper into the canyon, giving amazing views of the area. It's a short trail, but with a decent ascent.

Horse Spring Trail Spur
Moderate – (1.0 mi / 1.6 km), round trip, allow 30 - 45 minutes

This is a spur trail from the Canyon Overlook Trail that heads into the upper canyon. Occasionally wild horses have been spotted here. Look for the spur right before the Canyon Overlook Trail begins its loop back to the trailhead.

Looking down into the Kershaw - Ryan oasis

Elgin Schoolhouse State Historic Park

Official Park Website:

- http://parks.nv.gov/parks/elgin-schoolhouse-state-historic-site

Visitor Center:

- None in park, contact (775) 726-3564, tours by reservation only

Park Accessibility:

- Okay for 2WD and RVs
- Day Use Only

Experience Level:

- Family Friendly

Camping in Park:

- None

Lodging and Dining in Park:

- None

Nearest Town with Amenities:

- Caliente, NV is 20 mi / 32 km from the park.

Getting There:

- From Caliente, NV: Take SR-317 South to Rainbow Canyon, in Lincoln County. Total distance is 20 mi / 32 km to park

What Makes Elgin Schoolhouse State Park Special

Elgin Schoolhouse SP protects a small one-room schoolhouse that operated from 1922 to 1967. This is a little building, which schooled several generations of children from grades one through eight and was the home of the Bradshaw family before coming under the preservation of the state. The schoolhouse was built by Reuben Bradshaw primarily out of necessity. Reuben's father, James Bradshaw homesteaded a ranch in the area in 1880. The Elgin Schoolhouse is a nice place to visit on the way to Kershaw-Ryan State Park, which manages Elgin, but to get a deeper experience, plan ahead to arrange a tour by calling the number listed in the "Quick Facts" section.

The Elgin Schoolhouse

Basin and Range National Monument

Quick Facts

Official Park Website:

- http://www.blm.gov/nv/st/en/prog/nlcs_new/Basin_ and_Range_National_Monument.html

Visitor Center:

- None in park, contact: Ely District Office, 702 N. Industrial Way, HC 33 Box 33500, Ely, NV 89301, Phone: (775) 289-1800

Park Accessibility:

- 4WD recommended
- Day and Overnight Use

Experience Level:

- Experienced Hiker – Backcountry Hiker

Camping in Park:

- No designated campground in park. Dispersed camping is allowed throughout all BLM-administered lands within the monument.

Lodging and Dining in Park:

- None

Nearest Town with Amenities:

- Caliente, NV is 83 mi / 134 km from park.

Getting There:

- From Caliente, NV: take US 93 South to NV-318 North to Mail Summit Road.

A great place to lose yourself

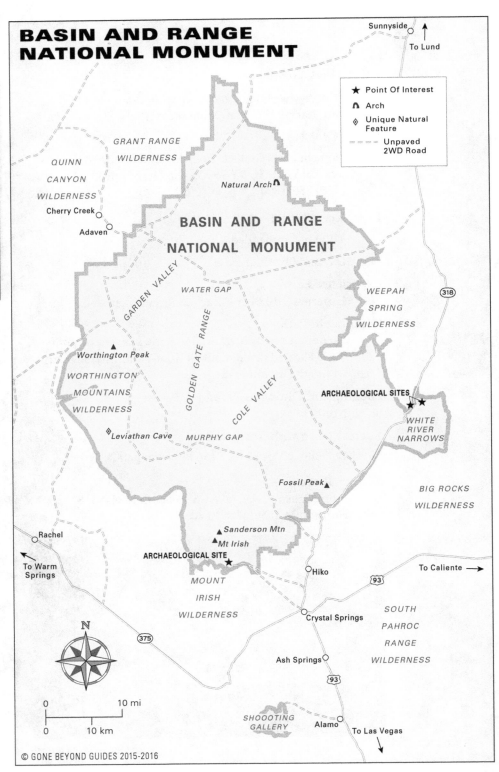

BASIN AND RANGE NATIONAL MONUMENT

EASTERN NEVADA

Basin and Range

Sunnyside
To Lund

Legend:
- ★ Point Of Interest
- ⋂ Arch
- ⬦ Unique Natural Feature
- --- Unpaved 2WD Road

GRANT RANGE WILDERNESS

QUINN CANYON WILDERNESS

Cherry Creek
Adaven

Natural Arch ⋂

BASIN AND RANGE NATIONAL MONUMENT

GARDEN VALLEY

WATER GAP

WEEPAH SPRING WILDERNESS

318

GOLDEN GATE RANGE

Worthington Peak ▲

WORTHINGTON MOUNTAINS WILDERNESS

COLE VALLEY

⬦ Leviathan Cave

MURPHY GAP

ARCHAEOLOGICAL SITES ★★

WHITE RIVER NARROWS

Fossil Peak ▲

BIG ROCKS WILDERNESS

Rachel

To Warm Springs

Sanderson Mtn ▲
▲ Mt Irish

ARCHAEOLOGICAL SITE ★

Hiko

To Caliente →

MOUNT IRISH WILDERNESS

93

Crystal Springs

SOUTH PAHROC RANGE WILDERNESS

375

N

Ash Springs

93

0   10 mi
0   10 km

SHOOOTING GALLERY

Alamo

To Las Vegas

© GONE BEYOND GUIDES 2015-2016

What Makes Basin and Range National Monument Special

- One of the newest national monuments in the United States

- Over 700,000 acres of pristine wilderness

- Finding complete solitude within open valleys grasslands and big skies

Basin and Range is new, created in July of 2015 by President Barack Obama. Being new has its upsides, namely in that visitors here are able to experience the park before it becomes known and developed. There are but a few unpaved roads and a smattering of undeveloped trails, meaning that the wilderness is yours to explore.

Highlights within the park include three archeological districts, the Mount Irish Archeological Site, the White River Narrows Archeological District, and the Shooting Gallery Petroglyph Area. White River has a fascinating collection of rock art that is both varied and abundant. Shooting Gallery is thought to have been a spot for driving game to the ancestral hunters. The rock art here is diverse, showing art styles from the Fremont, Pahranagat, and Great Basin people.

Then there is the Worthington Mountains Wilderness Area. This is a very different land of sharply eroded limestone mountains with caves to explore and 2,100-year-old ancient bristlecone pine forests. Leviathan Cave is the largest of the spelunking opportunities, with a gapping mouth 100 feet high by 180 feet wide. This leads to large chambers and fantastic ice formations as well as a large selection of cave formations. Note that you are on your own here, this cave is primarily for experienced spelunkers.

There is very little official documentation created for the park at this point in time. If Basin and Range National Monument sounds interesting after reading this, your next step is to contact the BLM managing office, which is in Ely. There number is (775) 289-1800.

Pull off and explore, the park is yours

Cathedral Gorge State Park

Quick Facts

Official Park Website:
- http://parks.nv.gov/parks/cathedral-gorge/

Visitor Center:
- None in park, contact: (775) 728-4460

Park Accessibility:
- Okay for 2WD and RVs
- Day and Overnight Use

Experience Level:
- Family Friendly – Casual Hiker

Camping in Park:
- Total of 22 T/RV sites, drinking water, flush toilets, showers, hookups, first come-first served

Lodging and Dining in Park:
- None

Nearest Town with Amenities:
- Caliente, NV is 15 mi / 24 km from park

Getting There:
- From St George, UT: Take UT-18 North to UT-56 West to NV-319 West to Cathedral Gorge State Park Road. Total distance is 98 mi / 158 km to park.

Namesake monoliths

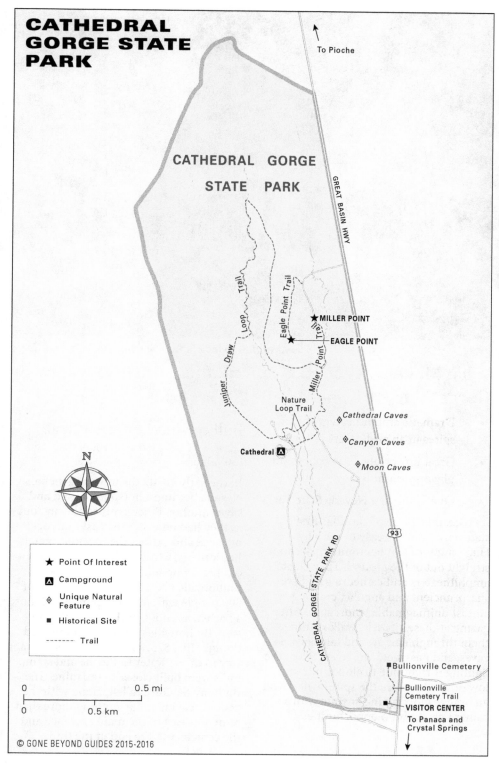

CATHEDRAL GORGE STATE PARK

CATHEDRAL GORGE
STATE PARK

To Pioche

GREAT BASIN HWY

Loop Trail

Eagle Point Trail

★ MILLER POINT

★ EAGLE POINT

Miller Point Trail

Juniper Draw

Nature
Loop Trail

Cathedral ◬

◇ Cathedral Caves

◇ Canyon Caves

◇ Moon Caves

93

CATHEDRAL GORGE STATE PARK RD

N

★ Point Of Interest

◬ Campground

◇ Unique Natural
   Feature

■ Historical Site

------- Trail

■ Bullionville Cemetery

Bullionville
Cemetery Trail

VISITOR CENTER

To Panaca and
Crystal Springs

0   0.5 mi

0   0.5 km

© GONE BEYOND GUIDES 2015-2016

Some of the eroded bluffs to be found in Cathedral Gorge

What Makes Cathedral Gorge State Park Special

- Dramatic amphitheaters of rock spires in an arid desert setting

- Great unworldly desert photography opportunities

- One of the first Nevada State Parks

It's true, this is one of Nevada's first state parks, and it's easy to see why. Huge spires of soft bentonite rock shoot straight out of the ground. They create amphitheaters and cathedrals that are sharp, ancient and angular, creating almost unimaginable landscapes. After gazing at these citadels, walk within them through narrow and tall canyons, caves, and passages. Moreover, when the lighting is right due to clouds or a sun low on the horizon, the spires will reflect an orange glow, giving anyone with a camera great photo opportunities.

Hiking Cathedral Gorge State Park

Bullionville Cemetery Trail
Easy – (0.4mi / 0.6 km), round trip, allow 30 minutes

In the early 1870's the town of Pioche, Nevada became a hotspot for gold and silver mining. Pioche mined the ore, but as they had no water to crush the rock material and extract the precious metals, Bullionville, which had a water source, did the stamp milling. The town of Bullionville had a heyday population of 500 people with five stamp mills, saloons, a barber, a school, and even a railroad stop. Bullionville's days were numbered though. By 1875, someone figured out a way to divert water to Pioche and stamp mills were built closer to the mine. The Bullionville railroad left, along with the people, leaving today nothing more than remnants east of the main entrance and the cemetery at the end of the trail.

Nature Loop

Easy – (0.5 mi / 0.8 km), round trip, allow 30 minutes

The Nature Loop is a great way for visitors in the campground area to walk to the caves and narrow slot ravines. This trail is relatively flat and can be potentially a great way to see wildlife in the early evening or morning hours.

Juniper Draw Loop

Moderate – (3.0mi / 4.8 km), round trip, allow 2 hours

Juniper Draw Loop parallels Miller Point Trail for less than a quarter mile before going off into the remote sections of the park. The trail itself is relatively flat, following alongside the spires that have made Cathedral Gorge so amazing. The hike returns by following a dry wash back to where you started. The trail is great for seeing the rugged nature of the area, giving great views of the spires as well as ponderosa pines and the occasional animal tracks. The lighting for this hike is best in the early morning and late afternoon, where the low angle of the sun brings out the rich colors in the rock.

Miller Point Trail

Moderate – (2.0 mi / 3.2 km), round trip, allow 1 hour to 90 minutes

Miller Point is a there and back trail giving a great view of the Cathedral Gorge. There is a bit of elevation gain on this trail, which can make for strenuous walking. There is little to no vegetation in this Mar's like landscape. The area is desolate and stark, which brings to the eye a sentiment of beauty founded in what is not there. There are also some opportunities for caving and slot ravine explorations. Look for the obvious spur trails but as the rock is soft, it's not great for climbing and doing so only erodes the area unnaturally.

Eagle Point Trail

Moderate to Strenuous – (1.6 mi / 2.6 km), round trip, allow 1 hour

Eagle Point is another there and back trail leading to great views of the Cathedral Gorge and is typically done as an extension of the Miller Point Trail. Again, moon like landscapes with lots of spur trail explorations to be found. This trail has some strenuous segments.

Some of the eroded bluffs to be found in Cathedral Gorge

Echo Canyon State Park

Quick Facts

Official Park Website:

- http://parks.nv.gov/parks/echo-canyon-state-park/

Visitor Center:

- None in park, contact (775) 962-5103

Park Accessibility:

- Okay for 2WD and RVs
- Day and Overnight Use

Experience Level:

- Family Friendly – Casual Hiker

Camping in Park:

- Echo Canyon Campground: 33 T/RV, drinking water, flush toilet, no hookups, dump station, first come-first served

Lodging and Dining in Park:

- None

Nearest Town with Amenities:

- Pioche, NV is 13 mi / 21 km from the park.

Getting There:

- From Las Vegas, NV: Take US-93 North to Echo Dam Road in Pioche, NV. Total distance is 188 mi / 303 km to park.

Echo Canyon Reservoir

What Makes Echo Canyon State Park Special

- Close to Cathedral Gorge, Beaver Dam and Kershaw-Ryan State Parks
- Boat ramps, fishing, camping and general relaxation are the key ingredients of this park
- Great scenery located about three hours north of Las Vegas, NV

The best part of Echo Canyon is what it isn't. This is a place of relaxation versus adventure, of dipping your toe in cool waters versus navigating down some Class 4 slickrock. You can pull up, get the campsite set up to your liking, grab a drink, and just start relaxing. The place offers 33 campsites, a boat ramp, a stocked lake and one trail across its 65 acres. Echo Canyon allows one to kick back, catch some fish, and not think about much of anything.

Hiking in Echo Canyon State Park

Ash Canyon Trail
Moderate – (2.5 mi / 4.0 km), round trip, allow 90 minutes

This hike starts with a 300-foot climb over one third mile to the valley's rim and then descends into the volcanic walls of Ash Canyon. The highlight here is the canyon itself, which is tall and brooding, the perfect hide out for a western bandit. The trail ends by dropping into Echo Canyon, which can be hiked back to the trailhead, making a loop. A brochure can be picked up that explains some of the features along the way at various numbered posts.

The lazy landscape of Echo Canyon State Park

Spring Valley State Park

Official Park Website:

- http://parks.nv.gov/parks/ spring-valley-state-park/

Visitor Center:

- None in park, contact (775) 962-5102

Park Accessibility:

- Okay for 2WD and RVs
- Day and Overnight Use

Experience Level:

- Family Friendly

Camping in Park:

- Horsethief Gulch Campground: 37 T/RV, drinking water, re-strooms, showers, no hookups, first come-first served
- Ranch Campground: 7 T/RV, drinking water, restrooms, no hookups, first come-first

Lodging and Dining in Park:

- None

Nearest Town with Amenities:

- Pioche, NV is 21 mi / 34 km from the park.

Getting There:

- From St George, UT: Take UT-18 North to UT-56 West to NV-319 West to NV-322 E/State Route 322 to Eagle Valley Road. Total distance is 128 mi / 206 km to park

What Makes Spring Valley State Park Special

Another in the grouping of state parks off Highway 93, north of Las Vegas. Like Echo Canyon, Kershaw-Ryan, and Beaver Dam State Parks, the prime motivation for coming here is water recreation and just plain getting in a little rest and relaxation (at last). There are many campsites, the stocked Eagle Valley Reservoir, and a boat launch area.

The one differentiation of this park is the Historic Millet Ranch House and other Mormon homestead buildings. The Millet House doubles as the park's headquarters. There is a museum that houses some of the artifacts and one can stroll around the surrounding outbuildings.

Spring Valley Entrance

Quick Facts

Official Park Website:

- http://www.nps.gov/grba

Visitor Center:

- (775) 234-7331

- Lehman Caves Tours Advance Ticket Sales (775) 234-7517

Park Accessibility:

- Okay for 2WD and RVs

- Day and Overnight Use

Experience Level:

- Family Friendly – Experienced Hiker

Camping in Park:

- Lower Lehman Creek Campground: 11 T/RV, open year round, drinking water in summer only, no hook-ups, some pull-thru sites

- Upper Lehman Creek Campground: 22 T/RV, open seasonally, drinking water in summer, no pull-thru sites

- Wheeler Peak Campground: 37 T/RV, open seasonally, drinking water in summer, no pull thru sites, limited RV spaces, road to campground not recommended for vehicles longer than 24 feet.

- Baker Creek Campground: 38 T/RV, open seasonally, drinking water in summer, no pull thru sites

- Strawberry Creek Campground: 8 T, open year round, no water, 2 group sites

Lodging and Dining in Park:

- None

Nearest Town with Amenities:

- Baker, NV, 5 is mi / 8 km from park.

Getting There:

- From Baker, NV: Take NV-488 West 5 is mi / 8 km to park entrance.

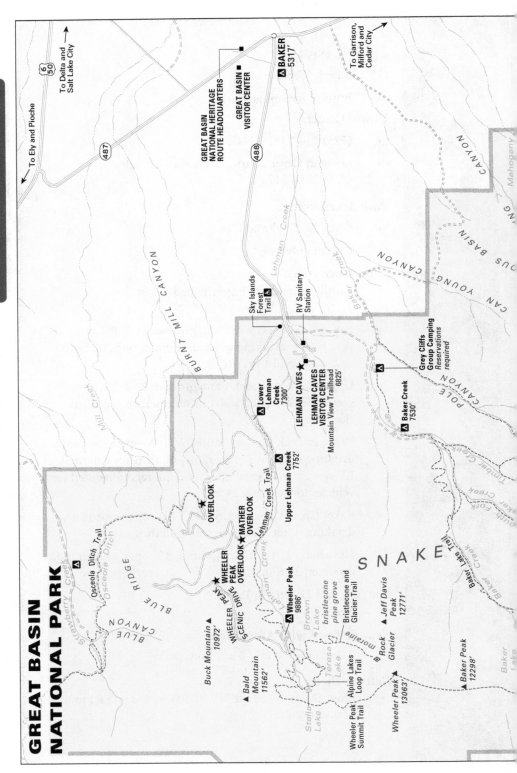

GREAT BASIN
NATIONAL PARK

To Ely and Pioche

To Delta and
Salt Lake City

6
50

487

488

To Garrison,
Milford and
Cedar City

BAKER
5317'

GREAT BASIN
NATIONAL HERITAGE
ROUTE HEADQUARTERS

GREAT BASIN
VISITOR CENTER

Lehman Creek

Baker Creek

MUNGO CANYON

CAN YOUNG CANYON

POLE CANYON

Mahogany

BURNT MILL CANYON

Mill Creek

Sky Islands
Forest Trail

RV Sanitary
Station

Grey Cliffs
Group Camping
Reservations
required

LEHMAN CAVES
VISITOR CENTER
Mountain View Trailhead
6825'

Lower
Lehman
Creek
7300'

Baker Creek
7530'

Upper Lehman Creek
7752'

OVERLOOK

MATHER
OVERLOOK

WHEELER
PEAK
OVERLOOK

Lehman Creek Trail

Osceola Ditch Trail

Osceola Ditch

Strawberry Creek

BLUE RIDGE

BLUE CANYON

WHEELER PEAK SCENIC DRIVE

Buck Mountain
10972'

Bald
Mountain
11562'

Wheeler Peak
9886'

Brown
Lake

bristlecone
pine grove

Bristlecone and
Glacier Trail

Rock
Glacier

Jeff Davis
Peak
12771'

SNAKE

Timber Creek

South Fork Baker Creek

Baker Creek Trail

Baker Lake Trail

Stella
Lake

Terasa
Lake

Alpine Lakes
Loop Trail

Wheeler Peak
Summit Trail

Wheeler Peak
13063'

Baker Peak
12298'

Baker Lake

Moraine

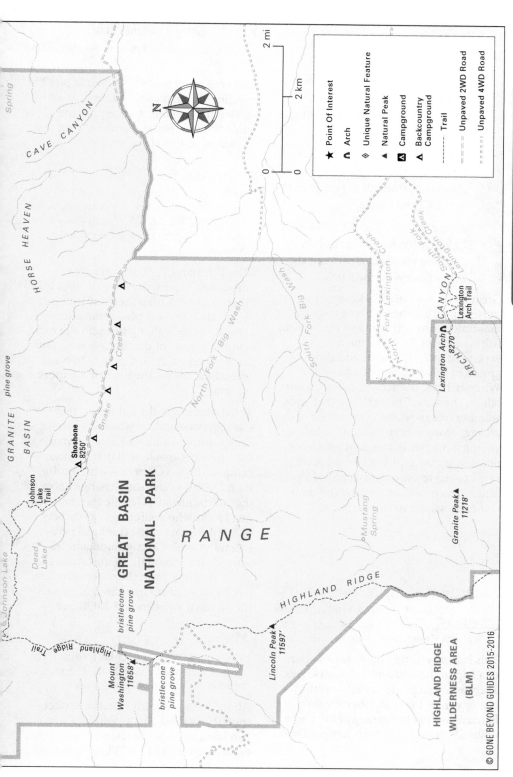

Legend

★ Point Of Interest
∩ Arch
◇ Unique Natural Feature
▲ Natural Peak
◪ Campground
▲ Backcountry Campground
------ Trail
═══ Unpaved 2WD Road
═══ Unpaved 4WD Road

Spring

CAVE CANYON

HORSE HEAVEN

GRANITE pine grove

BASIN

Snake Creek

▲ Shoshone
8250'

Johnson
Lake
Trail

Dead
Lake

Johnson Lake

Highland Ridge Trail

GREAT BASIN

NATIONAL PARK

bristlecone
pine grove

RANGE

Mount
Washington
11658'

bristlecone
pine grove

North Fork Big Wash

South Fork Big Wash

Mustang
Spring

HIGHLAND RIDGE

Lincoln Peak▲
11597'

Granite Peak▲
11218'

HIGHLAND RIDGE
WILDERNESS AREA
(BLM)

North Fork Lexington Creek

South Fork Lexington Creek

CANYON

Lexington Arch ∩
8270'

Lexington
Arch Trail

ARCH

N

0   2 km   2 mi

What Makes the Great Basin National Park Special

- With caves beneath the ground to bristlecone pines at the higher elevations, Great Basin NP contains incredible diversity
- The park's Basin and Range ecosystem is refreshingly unique and stands out from all the other parks in the Grand Circle
- Above the tree line, 13,063-foot (3,982 m) Wheeler Peak gives amazing views, plus you can see the curvature of the earth

Great Basin National Park's legacy started in 1922 when it was a national monument protecting the awe-inspiring Lehman Caves. In 1986, the area was expanded to 77,180 acres and protects groves of bristlecone pines as well as Wheeler Peak, the second tallest mountain in the state. The park is a true gem, whether one is brushing up smells of desert sage along a meadow trail or hiking amongst the twisted ancient bristlecone pines, whether exploring breathtaking caves or the treeless landscapes of alpine tundra, each section is vastly different and each wholly magnificent.

Hiking Great Basin National Park

Mountain View Nature Trail

Easy – (0.3 mi / 0.5 km), round trip, allow 30 minutes, elev. Δ: 80 ft / 24 m, trailhead at Rhodes Cabin near visitor center

This is a great little hike to take as part of a trip to the adjacent Lehman Caves. There is a trail guide available at the visitor center that describes the flora and fauna as well as the geology of the area as it winds through a pinyon juniper forest.

Sky Islands Forest Trail

Easy – (0.4 mi / 0.6 km), round trip, allow 30 minutes

This trail is flat and wheelchair accessible, winding through conifer forests at an elevation of 9800 feet. Interpretative signs guide the way. Bring warm clothing and sunscreen at this elevation.

Lehman Creek Trail

Moderate to Strenuous – (6.8 mi / 10.9 km), round trip, allow 4-5 hours, elev. Δ: 2,050 ft / 625 m, trailheads at Wheeler Peak and Upper Lehman Creek campground.

The Lehman Creek Trail is a true mountain experience hike. Within this there and back hike there are multiple tributaries to cross plus some nice waterfalls while walking through the rocky conifer forests of the Snake Range. This is the creek of the last glacier in Nevada, which makes the hike all the more special.

The trail starts at the Lehman Creek Campground and ends at the Wheeler Peak Campground, which could make for a nice backpacking trip from one camp to the next. There is a bit more than 2,000 feet elevation change between the two trailheads. Despite the elevation, most folks who are just going one way (4.4 miles) start at the trailhead near Lehman Creek Campground and hike towards the mountain to maximize the views. Starting from the other direction has its own advantages though, namely the fact that you descend 2,000 feet.

Alpine Lakes Loop Trail

Moderate – (2.7 mi / 4.3 km), round trip, allow 2 hours, elev. Δ: 600 ft / 183 m, trailhead at Bristlecone parking area

Alpine Lakes is pretty much a perfect trail. It is indeed a loop, winding past two lakes right below the tree line, giving expansive views of Mt Wheeler. Hiking

Lehman Caves

The park offers two different tours of the caves, the Lodge Room Tour and the Grand Palace Tour. Tours are offered year round, with different availability depending on the season. The park rangers lead each tour and explain the history, geology, and ecology of Lehman Caves. The caves are at a constant 50° F (10° C), so bring a warm layer. In addition, the caves can be slippery in spots, so bring shoes with good traction. Cave photography is allowed but may at times be at the discretion of the ranger.

Tickets are required to take the tours and must be purchased in advance. It is possible to purchase tickets at the Lehman Caves Visitor Center, but it is strongly recommended to reserve your place by phone at (775) 234-7517. Phone sales are available during normal business hours (9AM–4PM PST) Monday through Friday. Visitors can buy tickets up to 30 days in advance. Once purchased, they are nonrefundable and are subject to forfeiture if not picked up at least 15 minutes prior to tour time.

There is a question/answer screening process that visitors will need to go through prior to entering the caves. This process is meant to reduce the spread of White Nose Syndrome (that's "nose" not "noise"). This is a skin infection found in hibernating bats that appears to have been introduced to North America from Europe. The infection, which only affects bats, is seen as a cause in the increase in bat mortality. In general, visitors who have not yet been in a mine or cave can continue on to their tour. Visitors who have been in another mine or cave must change clothes, and cameras must be wiped down with decontaminating wipes. Shoes must also be decontaminated, which involves soaking them in a solution bath for 5

Inside the Lehman Caves

minutes. The wipes and solution are offered by the park. Bottom line, don't wear or bring anything from another cave or mine system, and you will be fine.

Lodge Room Tour

This tour lasts about an hour, and ticket prices are $8 for adults and $4 for children 5–15 (under five is free). The Lodge Room tour includes the Music Room, Lodge Room, and Gothic Palace sections, covering everything over 0.4 miles round-trip. Since this is the shortest tour in both duration and distance, it is the most recommended for families with younger children. Tours are limited to 20 visitors at a time.

Grand Palace Tour

This tour lasts 90 minutes and ticket prices are $10 for adults and $5 for children 5–15. Children under five are not allowed (except from November to February). The Grand Palace Tour covers the same sections as the Lodge Room Tour. Additionally, the Grand Palace and Inscription Room sections are also included. The Grand Palace section is where the famous and widely photographed Parachute Shield is located. This tour is also limited to 20 visitors. Bottom line, if you have a child under five, consider the Lodge Room Tour. Otherwise, spend the extra couple of bucks and take the Grand Palace Tour.

counter clockwise, Stella Lake is first up and gives the best views of the surrounding mountain side, followed by smaller Teresa Lake. Along the way are groves of quaking Aspens, the gentle Lehman Creek, large conifer trees amongst an ecosystem carved by ancient glaciers.

Wheeler Peak Summit Trail

Strenuous – (8.6 mi / 13.8 km), round trip, allow 5-7 hours, elev. Δ: 2,900 ft / 884 m, trailhead at Summit Trail parking area

Wheeler Peak is a very attainable summit in the summer but does require some planning beforehand. The bottom line is to be off the peak before the afternoon thunderstorms come and start hitting the highest, most exposed location in eastern Nevada.

The easiest way to ensure this is to plan to be at the trailhead by 7am. Not waking up at 7am mind you, up, packed, energized and ready to hike by 7am. Doing this will ensure you are down before the afternoon storms hit, should they decide to. The other tip is to pack easily digested food for snacks and lunch. At just over 13,000 feet, there isn't a lot of oxygen to help digest food. One way to combat this is to avoid eating foods that take tons of oxygen to digest such as proteins, and complex carbs. Stick to simple carbs for the trip and eat a big meal afterwards. Cramping at altitude is never fun. Caffeine can also be helpful for energy and stamina at altitude.

All this "what to do at high altitude" may seem like overkill, but for the many that are coming in from living for years at closer to sea level, the effects of high altitude can be real and tend to strike without warning or forgiveness. The safest path still holds, which is to acclimate first. Altitude sickness symptoms are nonspecific and affect each person differently. If you feel overly fatigued, have a loss of appetite, feel like vomiting and generally just "can't go on", then come back down. Work out with your hiking partner beforehand so that you both can assess each other's symptoms. Also, agree on your abortion strategy prior to heading up. Being fully able to continue while your partner cannot can be frustrating, but safety should always come before bagging a summit at any cost. Given that one of the symptoms of altitude sickness is disorientation and inability to think clearly, the best plan in this situation is to come down together. That said, most folks climb up Wheeler Peak without any issues other than shortness of breath, which is normal. Don't let altitude sickness keep you from the attempt, simply be aware of it before heading up.

The trail starts through the forest canopy along the Alpine Lakes Loop Trail heading towards Stella Lake. Just before hitting the lake, there is a right hand turn off for the peak. Continue climbing gently up the sloping meadows of Bald Mountain, eventually moving onto a ridge that takes you above the tree line.

Great Basin National Park

Upper Lehman Creek

From here, you enter onto a rocky moraine that you must navigate through before climbing two increasingly steeper pitches to the summit. The summit itself is broad and worth exploration. The views are, as expected, spectacular in every direction. To the east is Jeff Davis Peak at 12,771 feet and to the south is Baker Peak, standing at 12, 298 feet.

Note that in the winter, Wheeler Peak is packed with snow and should only be attempted by experienced mountaineers).

Bristlecone Trail

Moderate to Strenuous due to elevation– (2.8 mi / 4.5 km), round trip, allow 2 hours, elev. Δ: 600 ft / 183 m, trailhead at Summit Trail parking area

There are several groves of bristlecone pine in Great Basin National Park. This trail near Wheeler Peak offers the easiest journey to visit them. There is about 600 feet of elevation gain, which combined with the elevation, can be considered a strenuous hike. Take your time if you can't find a sustainable cadence of breath.

The hike is definitely worth the journey. There is something magical about a grove of bristlecone pines. They grow near the

tree line and have been dated at living up to (and perhaps beyond) 4,600 years. To put this into perspective, we mere humans will see around 27,000 sunrises in our lifetime and of those, most of us will miss all but a handful of them. A bristlecone pine will see over 1.5 million sunrises and sunsets. They will have seen the frozen white of winter transform into the renewal of spring some 400,000 times. While they are but trees, the feeling one gets when walking amongst these ancient beings is one of wisdom and humility. It is one of the more remarkable life moments to visit a grove of bristlecone pines and must be experienced firsthand.

Bristlecone and Glacier Trail

Strenuous due to elevation– (4.6 mi / 7.4 km), round trip, allow 4-5 hours, elev. Δ: 1,100 ft / 335 m, trailhead at Summit Trail parking area

Glacier Trail is the continuation of Bristlecone Trail to Nevada's only glacier. This little guy is the sole remnant of a period that ended some 10,000 years ago when the earth was several degrees cooler and glaciers amassed greater size and lower elevations. The glacier is as you might suspect, decreasing in size due to the warmer planetary climate and is estimated to become "extinct" in about 20 years. If you do go look around you. The entire mountain, including the very top of Wheeler Peak, was carved by glaciers. The gentle broad slopes and horn shape of Wheeler Peak are signatures of glacial forces. Wheeler Peak Glacier is the last of that era when the Ice Age shaped mountains with the incredible power of water.

Highland Ridge

Strenuous – (9.8 mi / 15.8 km), one way, allow 7 – 9 hours, elev. Δ: 2,900 ft / 890 m, trailhead at Summit Trail parking area

Looking for a bit more adventure than pulling up to a trailhead and hiking on an existing path? Consider the "Highland Ridge" route.

This route is part trail, part unmarked trekking, and is a great hike for those who are looking for some true adventure. The route climbs along the scenic mountain spine known as Highland Ridge. It starts up via the Wheeler Peak Summit Trail to the top of the 13,065-foot Wheeler Peak. From there, the journey goes off trail via the Highland Ridge to nearby Baker Peak standing at 12,298 feet. Continue towards Mt. Washington along the ridge, staying in a southward direction as you pass Baker Lake below.

The last peak on this journey is Mt. Washington. You will pick up a rather unmaintained trail near Johnson Lake and will continue on this trail for the remainder of the hike. Mt. Washington stands at 11,658 and also contains the largest grove of bristlecone pines in the park.

Essentially, what's being described here is a hike that bags three peaks in a backcountry alpine landscape within the most remote part of the park that has the added bonus of hiking amongst a rather remote grove of ancient bristlecone pines. Hiking really doesn't get much better than this.

There are several ways off the Highland Ridge. You could return the way you came, which is the only real option if you have one car. There are also trails to the east via Baker, Johnson and North Fork East Wash, which will require a shuttle car and like the "up and back' option, will make this a 20-mile journey.

There is one last way to exit off Mt Washington without having to hike any further. To the west of the mountain is a parking area. You could leave a shuttle car there. That said, the road to the Mt. Washington parking lot is so rough the park service doesn't even put it on the map. The road is not horrible, but does contain a lot of switchbacks and should be left to an experienced driver with a decent high clearance 4-wheel drive vehicle.

Wheeler Peak Grove

Osceola Ditch Trail

Easy – (0.6 mi / 1.0 km), round trip, allow 45 minutes, elev. Δ: 100 ft / 30 m, trailhead at Rhodes Cabin near visitor center

This is a there and back interpretive trail through conifer forests that leads to a bit of gold mining history. In 1872, gold was discovered in the area and within ten years, the town of Osceola was flourishing. There was but one problem, not enough water to run the placer mines. Placer mining is done by shooting water at a hillside and then mining the slurry of mud material downstream.

The answer was an 18-mile water diversion ditch (plus an initial ditch that was 16 miles long but didn't produce enough water, oops). In fact, the whole operation was a failure. The cost to build the ditches was far more than the gold they recovered once they got everything working. Thus, as most tales of gold mining end, by 1905, the Osceola mine had only a trickle of activity.

Lexington Arch Trail

The trail to the Lexington Arch and the dirt road leading to it are closed due to fire damage until further notice. Inquire at the visitor center for latest updates.

Baker Lake Trail

Strenuous – (12.0 mi / 19.3km), round trip, allow 7-9 hours, elev. Δ: 2,620 ft / 800 m, trailhead at end of Baker Creek Road

With a 2,600-foot elevation gain and a distance of 12 miles, the Baker Lake Trail is more of a backpacking trail for many. It can be done as a day hike and will reward the hiker with a superb outback experience to an alpine lake. The trail starts at the Baker Creek Campground (ensure you are on Baker Creek Trail and not South Fork Baker Creek Trail). The trail climbs steadily up Baker Creek, which holds a host of alpine flowers and other flora along the way. As you climb, the forest thins out before diverting south up a set of well-marked switchbacks. There are plenty of cairns to mark the final leg to Baker Lake.

The lake itself holds some native trout, which may have attracted an angler, or two. It is possible to take an unmaintained connector trail to Johnson Lake and return via that trail, which will add

an additional 0.6 miles to create a loop (13.1 miles, 21.1 km total). Do ask at the visitor center prior to attempting this route, as the divide may be impassable due to snow. Even with snow, walking up to the top of the divide provides exceptional views.

South Fork Baker Creek/ Johnson Lake

Strenuous – (11.2 mi / 18.0 km), round trip, allow 7-9 hours, elev. Δ: 2,740 ft / 835 m, trailhead on Baker Lake Trail

South Fork Baker Creek Trail is a split from the Baker Lake Trail, which follows the South Fork of Baker Creek close to the headwaters before heading up and over a divide to join the Johnson Lake Trail. Once on the Johnson Lake Trail, look for the Johnson Lake Mill Historic Site, which contains intact cabins and other out structures. The wooded setting makes for great photo opportunities at both the mine site and the lake.

Johnson Lake Trail (from Snake Creek)

Strenuous – (7.4 mi / 11.9 km), round trip, allow 6 - 7 hours, elev. Δ: 2,420 ft / 738 m, trailhead at end of Snake Creek Road

The Johnson Lake Trail can be accessed by following along the Snake Creek from the Snake Creek Road trailhead. This route is shorter, but also steeper, connecting with Johnson Lake Trail. From here, the trail passes the Johnson Lake Mill Historic Site before heading to the lake. Johnson Lake is named after Alfred Johnson who discovered tungsten along the eastern slopes of Snake Creek. Alfred set up the Johnson Lake Mine in 1912. Evidence of the miner's operations is still quite prevalent. All of the mineshafts in the area go very deep and are extremely dangerous. Do not enter them.

Cave Lake State Park

Quick Facts

Official Park Website:

- http://parks.nv.gov/parks/cave-lake-state-park/

Visitor Center:

- (775) 296-1505 (leave message only)

Park Accessibility:

- Okay for 2WD and RVs
- Day and Overnight Use

Experience Level:

- Family Friendly – Casual Hiker

Camping in Park:

- Elk Flat Campground: 75 T/RV sites, open in season, drinking water, flush toilets, showers, no hookups, first come-first served
- Lake View Campground: 17 T/RV, open all year, drinking water, flush toilets, showers, no hookups, first come-first served

Lodging and Dining in Park:

- None

Nearest Town with Amenities:

- Ely, NV is 13 mi / 21 km from park.

Getting There:

- From St George, UT: Take UT-18 North to UT-56 West to NV-319 West to US-93 North to State Highway 486. Total distance is 213 mi / 343 km to park.

The peaceful scenery of Cave Lake

What Makes Cave Lake Special

- Pleasant high desert and lakeside scenery
- Great fishing, including brown trout
- The White Pine Fire and Ice Show, a winter ice sculpture event held in the park with fireworks and great local fun

Many come to Cave Lake for the fishing and boating. If you come mainly to hike, this means more chances to take in the views while having the trail all to yourself. This park offers lofty distant peaks that are often covered in snow as a backdrop to trails that are carved through high desert sagebrush. The park is at an elevation of 7,500 feet and does get good snow in the winter. In fact, each winter, the locals put on an ice sculpture contest, complete with fireworks that echo crisply against the surrounding mountain rock.

Hiking Cave Lake State Park

Twisted Pines Trail
Moderate – (4.1 mi / 6.6 km), one way, allow 2 – 3 hours

As of this writing, this is the newest trail to the park. The main purpose of the trail is to provide a longer loop from Steptoe Creek Trail around a basalt mesa named Square Top. This trail is as scenic as all of them and when combined, offers a decent 8.4-mile day hike.

Steptoe Creek Trail
Easy to Moderate – (1.6 mi / 2.6 km), one way, allow 45 minutes to 1 hour

Steptoe Creek is a favorite of anglers and provides an easy stroll across the creek via a series of footbridges. It's easy enough to make this a longer loop by combining with the Twisted Pines Trail to Cave Springs Trail (about 8.4 miles total if you take this route). The creek portion is more open than wooded.

Cave Springs Loop
Moderate to Strenuous – (4.9 mi / 7.9 km), round trip, allow 2 – 3 hours

The trail starts at the lower parking lot and heads into pinyon juniper forests of the Schell Creek Range. The trail ambles up and into the forest heading south east before descending to Cave Creek. From here, follow the creek back. This is a loop with some moderately strenuous climbing with a pleasant creek-side finish, which makes Cave Springs Loop a popular trail. Offers great views of the lake and surrounding mountainside.

Cave Overlook Trail
Strenuous – (3.8 mi / 6.1 km), round trip, allow 1 -2 hours

This is a fairly strenuous trail with a grade of 12% in some sections and climbing to a maximum elevation of 7,800 feet. The views of the lake and mountainside are certainly worth the workout. Head to the south of the lake on the paved road and look for a dirt road on your left. Climb steadily for about 1.8 miles before coming to the Twisted Pines Trail junction. Stay to your left and loop back to where you started.

High Roller Trail
Moderate – (2.1 mi / 3.4 km), one way, allow 1 hour

High Roller Trail is accessed via either the Twisted Pine Trail or Cave Overlook Trail. As a result, it offers a remote extension from either of these trails that when done correctly, forms a nice loop. This trail offers stunning views of the countryside and is one of the best hikes in the park as well as one the most remote.

Ward Charcoal Ovens State Park

Quick Facts

Official Park Website:

- http://parks.nv.gov/parks/ward-charcoal-ovens-state-historic-park/

Visitor Center:

- None in park, contact (775) 289-1693 (message only)

Park Accessibility:

- Okay for 2WD and RVs
- Day and Overnight Use

Experience Level:

- Family Friendly – Casual Hiker

Camping in Park:

- Willow Creek Campground: 15 T/RV, no drinking water, restrooms, no hookups, reservable by calling (775) 289-1693

Lodging and Dining in Park:

- None

Nearest Town with Amenities:

- Ely, NV is 21 mi / 34 km from park.

Getting There:

- From Ely, NV: Take US-50 East and turn right onto White Pine County Road 16. Total distance is 21 mi / 34 km to park.

Oven symmetry

What Makes Ward Charcoal Ovens State Park Special

- Relaxing high desert scenery with peaceful hikes

- Main feature are the bee hive shaped Ward charcoal ovens, some of the best preserved in the state

- Trying to find the related ghost town of Ward, a once thriving silver mine town that's been all but washed away by numerous flash floods

Ward Charcoal Ovens State Park offers a softer side of "ooh and awe". It's location in the high desert and the fact that most folks come for the charcoal ovens and not for the hiking, make this park a hidden gem. That said, the ovens themselves are amongst the best-preserved charcoal ovens in the western United States and offer great photography opportunities. There are six total and each are 30 feet high and 27 feet at the diameter, all shaped like bee hives.

Hiking Ward Charcoal Ovens State Park

All trails offer off the beaten path serenity amidst pinyon juniper high desert. Most trails are great for mountain biking and hiking as well as cross-country skiing in the winter. Be sure to bring water, none is provided at the trailhead. All trails start at the charcoal ovens.

Interpretive Loop

Easy – (0.6 mi / 1.0 km), round trip, allow 30 minutes

A short little loop that takes the visitor to Willow Creek and back.

Riparian Loop

Easy – (2.0 mi / 3.2 km), round trip, allow 1 hour

A longer trail that walks along the South Fork Willow Creek, cutting over to Willow Creek, and following it back to the trailhead. It is possible to fish for rainbow and brown trout along Willow Creek. This is a great trail for finding the perfect fishing hole.

Overlook Loop

Moderate – (0.9 mi / 1.4 km), round trip, allow 30 -45 minutes

At approximately one-mile total, this short loop climbs to give a bird's eye view of the ovens, surrounding creeks and the landscape.

Ridgeline Loop

Moderate – (1.6 mi / 2.6 km), round trip, allow 1 hour

This loop parallels much of Riparian Loop but with a little more variety by cutting west at South Fork Willow Creek and then crossing back to Willow Creek proper. Great hike for more solitude and experiencing the smells, sights, and sounds of the high desert countryside.

Campground Owens Trail

Easy – (0.6 mi / 1.0 km), one way, allow 30 minutes

Great route for campers wanting to see the charcoal ovens. On can use this trail to connect to any of the trails mentioned here.

Northwest Arizona

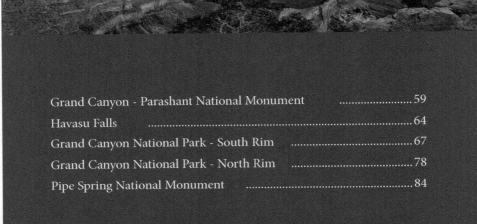

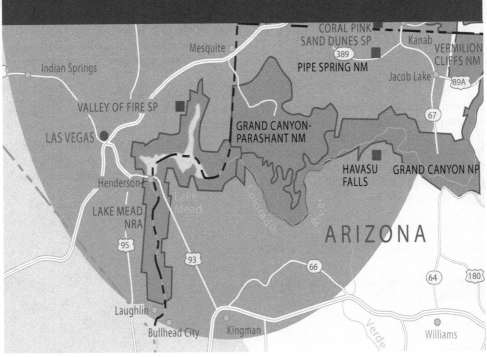

Quick Facts

Official Park Website:

- http://www.nps.gov/para

Visitor Center:

- None in park, contact: Public Lands Information Center (NPS, BLM, Forest Service), 345 East Riverside Drive, St. George, UT 84790, Phone: (435) 688-3200

- Note: it is strongly recommended visitors pick up a copy of the BLM Arizona Strip Visitor Map before entering. This map shows all roads along the Arizona Strip. Maps can be purchased at 345 E. Riverside Dr., St. George, UT 84790, or by calling (435) 688-3275.

Park Accessibility:

- 2WD, 4WD recommended, no paved roads in park

- Primarily Overnight Use

Experience Level:

- Experienced Hiker – Backcountry Hiker

Camping in Park:

- No developed campgrounds, backcountry camping with permit

Lodging and Dining in Park:

- None

Nearest Town with Amenities:

- Bullfrog, Antelope Point, and Halls Crossing are the closest areas within the park with amenities. Page, AZ is closest town to the southern section of the park

Getting There:

- From St. George, UT: Take I-15 South to Southern Pkwy to Mount Trumbull Loop for 62 mi / 100 to park entrance

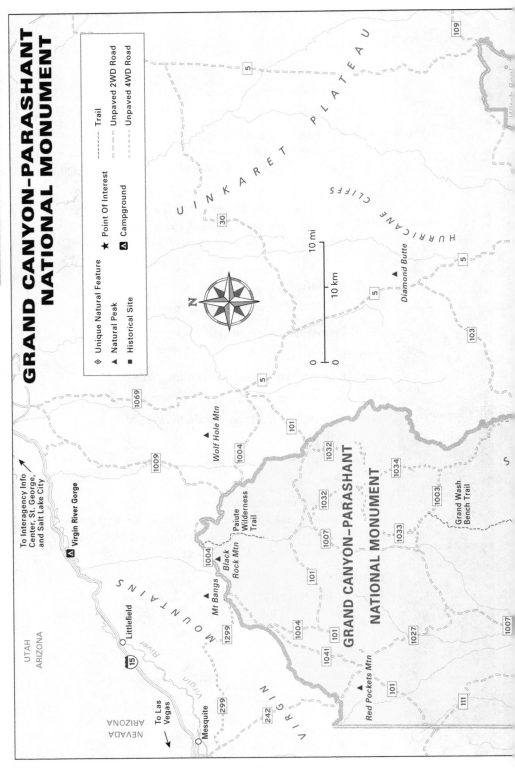

GRAND CANYON–PARASHANT
NATIONAL MONUMENT

◈ Unique Natural Feature   ★ Point Of Interest   ------ Trail
▲ Natural Peak   ▲ Campground   ---- Unpaved 2WD Road
■ Historical Site   ---- Unpaved 4WD Road

U I N K A R E T   P L A T E A U

H U R R I C A N E   C L I F F S

N

10 mi

10 km

0

0

▲ Diamond Butte

5

5

103

109

30

5

1069

1009

▲ Wolf Hole Mtn

1004

101

1032

1032

1007

101

1004

101

1034

1003

1033

GRAND CANYON–PARASHANT
NATIONAL MONUMENT

Grand Wash
Bench Trail

1027

1007

111

101

▲ Red Pockets Mtn

1041

1299

1004

▲ Mt Bangs

Black
Rock Mtn

Paiute
Wilderness
Trail

1004

⚑ Virgin River Gorge

To Interagency Info
Center, St. George,
and Salt Lake City

UTAH
ARIZONA

V I R G I N   M O U N T A I N S

15

River

Virgin

Littlefield ○

299

242

V I R G I N

Mesquite ○

NEVADA   ARIZONA
ARIZONA

To Las
Vegas

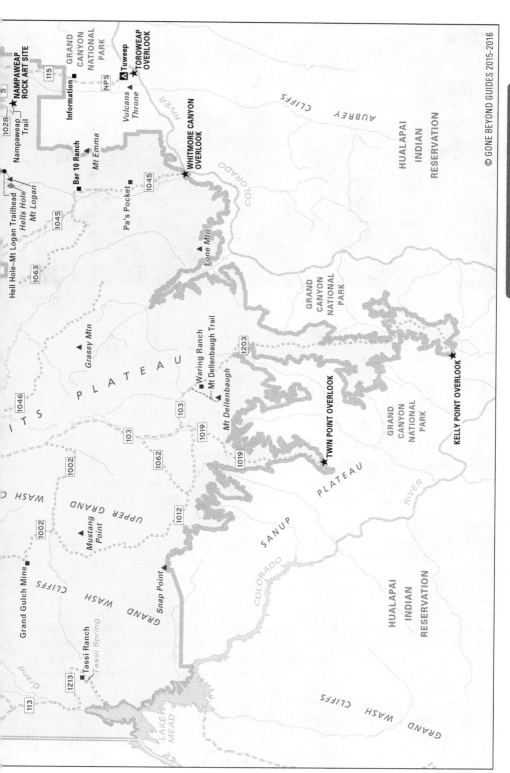

Grand Canyon - Parashant NORTHWEST ARIZONA

© GONE BEYOND GUIDES 2015-2016

61

One of the stunning views of Grand Canyon - Parashant National Monument

What Makes Grand Canyon-Parashant National Monument Special

- A rugged and isolated million-acre park with no paved roads
- Exceptional solitude in a Grand Canyon NP like setting
- Two forested peaks that give a very different perspective to the area

If isolation and solitude are what you are looking for, Parashant is the answer. This is a very large monument at just over one million acres, yet the park has no paved roads, lodges, or visitor center. This is a land where two sets of spares are the norm and the extra tanks of gas clinging to the side or your rig aren't just for show. It is a land that continues the story of the greatness of the Grand Canyon and covers the high plateau forests and desert grasslands that surround the canyon. The park holds three large wilderness areas, multiple plateaus, deep canyons and numerous washes.

Hiking Grand Canyon-Parashant NM

For all of these hikes, bring a topo map of the area to be hiked (and surrounding area), a good high clearance vehicle and the ability to self-sustain in the desert. Most of the hikes described below are remote and some are not maintained. Check with the BLM monument manager before any trip in this area to sync on local conditions. The BLM St. George office phone is (435) 688-3202.

Grand Wash Bench Trail

Strenuous – (20.0 mi / 32.2 km), round trip, full day trip or 2-day backpacking trip

The Grand Wash Bench Trail travels along a bench north to south within the 36,300-acre Grand Wash Cliffs Wilderness. Area scenery includes narrow canyons, two sets of towering cliffs and sandstone buttes. Ecologically, this hike travels through a transition zone and holds varied wildlife including bighorn sheep, the Gila monster, and the desert tortoise. Flora includes pinyon juniper forests and desert grasslands.

Mount Trumbull Trail

Moderate – (5.0 mi / 8.0 km), round trip, allow 4 hours

A pleasant hike to the top of an ancient shield volcano. The gradient up is mild after the initial ascent. The trail becomes route about 2/3 of the way up as the solid ground turns to deep cinders. Follow the paths of others and use a zigzag pattern to help make progress. There is a register at the true top of this 8,028-foot peak and no register at the false summit. From the top, there are sweeping views in every direction.

Hell Hole – Mount Logan Trail

Easy – (1.0 mi / 1.6 km), round trip, allow 1 hour

This is a short hike to the top of Mount Logan. Great majestic views into western Grand Canyon as well as southern Utah. The summit also gives a commanding view into Hell Hole, essentially the northern end of Grand Canyon's erosional artwork.

Nampaweap Rock Art Site

Easy – (1.0 mi / 1.6km), round trip, allow 30 minutes

Once thought to be a travel corridor, this short hike leads to hundreds of boulders containing thousands of petroglyphs left by ancient travelers over a 10,000-year period. Nampaweap means "foot canyon" in Paiute.

Mt. Dellenbaugh

Strenuous – (6.0 mi / 9.7 km), round trip, allow 4 hours

Similar to Mount Trumbull, this is another ancient shield volcano. The trail follows up an old converted jeep road to the top of this 7,012-foot peak. The peak has an interesting tie to the John Wesley Powell expedition. Three of Powell's team, William Dunn and brothers Oramel and Seneca Howland, decided they had enough of trying to be the first group of men to navigate down the Colorado River and left Powell. They hiked north through Separation Canyon and onto the Shivwits Plateau. William Dunn climbed Mount Dellenbaugh to get his bearings and inscribed both his name and year onto a rock. The three men were killed by the local Shivwits shortly thereafter. The historical graffiti can still be found with some exploration.

While this hike is one of two "official" hikes in the park (the other is Mount Trumbull), don't let that fool you. Getting to the trailhead requires traveling on dirt roads for nearly 90 miles. As repeatedly stated, Prashant is a remote land. However, for many, that's the point.

Looking south towards Grand Canyon from Mt Trumbull Wilderness

Havasu Falls

Quick Facts

Official Park Website: http://www.havasupai-nsn.gov/tourism.html

Visitor Center:

- Contact Havasupai Tourism at: P.O. Box 160 Supai, AZ, 86435, Phone: (928) 448-2121 or (928) 448-2141, (928) 448-2174, or (928) 448-2180

Park Accessibility:

- Okay for 2WD, RVs not recommended

- Primarily Overnight Use

Experience Level:

- Casual Hiker, some exposure

Camping in Park:

- Havasu Falls Campground: Reservations required, call Havasupai Tourism numbers listed above, (keep trying if no answer), 250T, drinking water, restrooms, no campfires, day ranger on duty in season

Lodging in Park:

- Havasupai Lodge, located on the trail 8 miles from trailhead in the town of Supai. Reservations required: (928) 448-2111 or (928) 448-2201.

Dining in Park:

- Supai Café, near Havasupai Lodge

Nearest Town with Amenities:

- Besides Supai, which is along the trail, Seligman, Arizona, 91 mi / 146 km from trailhead

Getting There:

- From Flagstaff: take US I-40 west to Historic Route 66 west at Seligman and turn right onto Indian Road 18 for 65 miles to trailhead at Hualapai Hilltop.

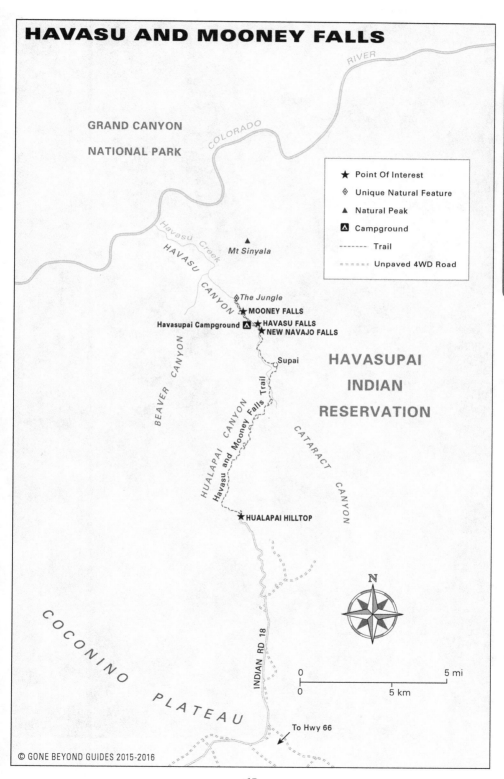

HAVASU AND MOONEY FALLS

GRAND CANYON

NATIONAL PARK

COLORADO RIVER

Legend:
- ★ Point Of Interest
- ◇ Unique Natural Feature
- ▲ Natural Peak
- 🅰 Campground
- ------- Trail
- ====== Unpaved 4WD Road

Havasu Creek

HAVASU CANYON

▲ Mt Sinyala

◇ The Jungle
★ MOONEY FALLS
Havasupai Campground 🅰 ★ HAVASU FALLS
★ NEW NAVAJO FALLS

BEAVER CANYON

Supai

HAVASUPAI
INDIAN
RESERVATION

HUALAPAI CANYON

Havasu and Mooney Falls Trail

CATARACT CANYON

★ HUALAPAI HILLTOP

N

COCONINO PLATEAU

INDIAN RD 18

| 0 | | 5 mi |
| 0 | | 5 km |

To Hwy 66

Havasu Falls

The sublime waters of Havasu Falls

What Makes Havasu and Mooney Falls Special

- Soft turquoise waters leading to healthy flowing 100 foot and 210 foot waterfalls in a peaceful canyon setting

- Ability to swim, camp and chill in this amazing area

- Getting a postcard to your family and friends partially via mules!

Within the entirety of the Grand Circle, Havasu and Mooney Falls are arguably the pinnacle of destinations. It is the soul of the Southwest, willing to accept all those that travel to it and yet the area continues to retain a serene simplicity and purity. If ever there should be an item at the top of your bucket list of places to go within the Grand Circle, this is that place.

Hiking Havasu and Mooney Falls

Havasu and Mooney Falls
Strenuous – (24.0 mi / 38.6 km), round trip, 2-day backpacking trip

First things first, get reservations and pay the fees. One will need to pay a $35 entrance fee plus an environment fee of $5, (each fee is per person). Camping is an additional $17 per person per night. Your entire party will be billed double this amount if you come without reservations, assuming there is availability. There is also a 10% tax on all purchases and a $5 Environmental Care Fee. Total for one night camping is $62.71 per person and $81.41 for two nights. The season opens on February 1st each year and 300 permits are given each day.

Now that you know the particulars on permits and camping, the next thing you will need is luck. The word is out on Havasu Falls and it is very difficult

to get a permit. The best approach is to mark your calendar for February 1st and then start dialing every number listed repeatedly until you get through. It is not unheard of for multiple folks trying from different phones to take several days to finally get through. As rough as this sounds, many do get through on the first day. The only good news here is this is the same process whether you are hiking alone or are booking for a professional tour company.

If you do have a group helping you to get the permits, have a plan A, B and C for dates and make sure you have a communication system for when you finally do get through. The season usually books out within weeks, but there is always hope that there will be a cancellation if you don't want to wait until next February to get in line.

Located within the Havasupai Reservation, the trip does get a lot of visitors during peak season. Start by finding a parking spot near the trailhead, which is situated about 1,000 feet off the canyon bottom. Right from the trailhead, you will see you are in a special place. The views down and around are amazing.

The hike heads steeply down to the valley floor via a series of switchbacks. There are plenty of mules along this trail and one needs to be especially diligent on this part. If you see mules coming, stick to the canyon wall side and not the cliff side. The mules often travel at a decent clip giving the backpacker little time to react. Hugging a wall in these instances tends to fair better than clinging to the edge of a cliff. This is especially true in a narrow section later on. The mules have the right of way on this trail.

Most of the hike travels along the wash, with great views of towering orange-red walls on either side. At about mile 7 into the journey, the trail narrows. Be especially aware of mules here. The hiking here is shadier and thus cooler unless you are doing this stretch at high noon.

The slot canyon opens into Havasu Creek and shortly thereafter to the peaceful village of the Supai People. The town holds 208 residents, give or take and is officially the most remote inhabited community in the lower 48. Besides flying in by helicopter (or as the locals call it, "cheating"), the only way in is via the Havasupai Trail. It is the last community in the United States to have its mail delivered by mule.

Havasu Falls are 2 miles from the town of Supai. These two miles deeper into the canyon are utterly sublime. The water is a light blue green turquoise. The distinctive hue comes from the strong reflection of the underlying limestone creek bed. It's not just the falls that are this color, the entire creek from Supai on are a gem like color of paradise found.

Havasu Falls and Mooney Falls further on are tall, roaring sheets of water and simply beyond words. Both are amazing and both must be seen. Getting to Mooney Falls requires a Class 3 descent to the bottom, some 210 feet below. Aids include a tunnel, ladders, handholds, railings, and footholds. This section is quite steep and exposed in areas and not for those that have a fear of heights. In addition, these areas become bottlenecks and one may have to stand in place as they wait for folks to come up or down. Finally, it should not be attempted when the conditions are wet or otherwise unfavorable, as sections can get very slippery. There is a campground in between the Havasu and Mooney Falls.

If you do want to send a post card home from Supai, note that the post office is closed on weekends. If you do go on a weekend, some locals are willing to mail it for you for a nominal fee. The novelty of mailing anything from the community is knowing that the first leg (pun intended) is by mule, the last community in the United States to move mail in this manner.

Another day in paradise

68

Grand Canyon National Park – South Rim

Quick Facts

Official Park Website:
http://www.nps.gov/grca

Visitor Center:

- General Visitor Information: (928) 638-7888
- Backcountry Information Center: (928) 638-7875

Park Accessibility:

- Okay for 2WD and RVs
- Day and Overnight Use

Experience Level:

- Family Friendly – Backcountry Hiker

Camping in Park:
Reservations strongly recommended at (877) 444-6777 or online at the http://www.recreation.gov/

- Mather Campground: 309 T/RV, open year round, drinking water, flush toilets, pull-thru sites, laundry and showers, no hookups, 30-foot total vehicle length, group sites available.
- Trailer Village RV: 80 RV, open year round, hookups, drinking water, flush toilets, accommodates vehicles up to 50 feet in length, pull-thru sites, shower and laundry
- Desert View: 50 T/RV, first come–first served, closed in winter, drinking water, restrooms, 30-foot total vehicle length, typically fills be early afternoon in summer.

Lodging in Park:

- 7 lodges in the South Rim, including Phantom Ranch. Go here for full details: http://www.nps.gov/grca/planyourvisit/lodging.htm. Reservations strongly recommended

Dining in Park:

- Multiple restaurants and markets for groceries. Go here for full details: http://www.nps.gov/grca/planyourvisit/restaurants.htm

Nearest Town with Amenities:

- Tusayan, AZ is less than 2 mi / 3 km from park

Getting There:

- From Flagstaff, AZ: take I-40 to US-180 North to South Rim park entrance

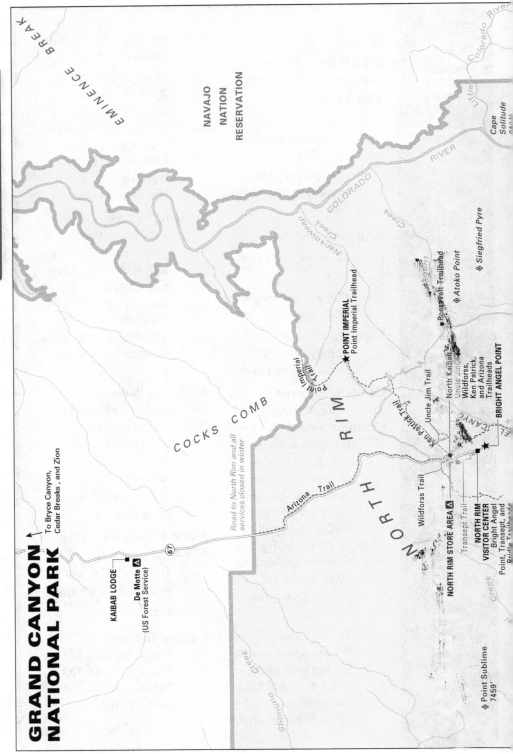

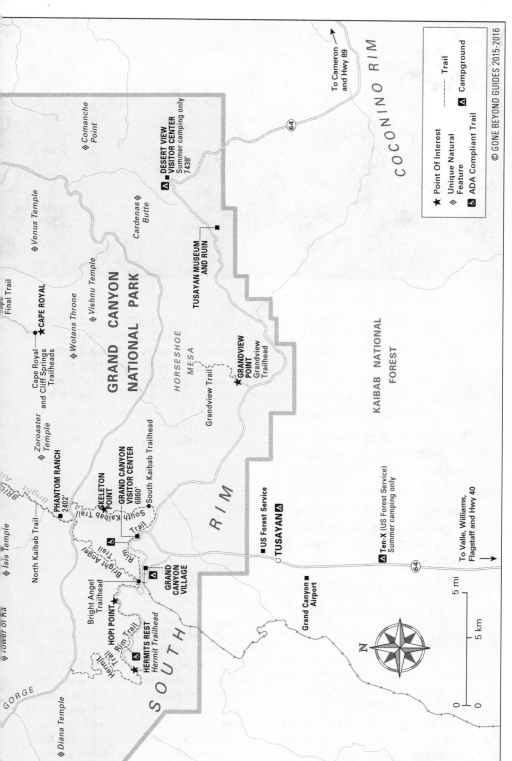

Grand Canyon - South Rim   NORTHWEST ARIZONA

© GONE BEYOND GUIDES 2015-2016

Legend:
- ★ Point Of Interest
- ◈ Unique Natural Feature
- ♿ ADA Compliant Trail
- ------- Trail
- ▲ Campground

To Cameron and Hwy 89

COCONINO RIM

64

◈ Comanche Point

★ DESERT VIEW VISITOR CENTER
Summer camping only
▲ 7438'

■ TUSAYAN MUSEUM AND RUIN

◈ Venus Temple

Cardenas ◈ Butte

★ CAPE ROYAL

GRAND CANYON NATIONAL PARK

Cape Royal and Cliff Springs Trailheads

◈ Wotans Throne

◈ Vishnu Temple

HORSESHOE MESA

★ GRANDVIEW POINT
Grandview Trailhead

Grandview Trail

Final Trail

◈ Zoroaster Temple

PHANTOM RANCH
2402'

SKELETON POINT
6860'

GRAND CANYON VISITOR CENTER

South Kaibab Trailhead

North Kaibab Trail

♿

GRAND CANYON VILLAGE

KAIBAB NATIONAL FOREST

◈ Isis Temple

South Kaibab Trail

Bright Angel Trail

Bright Angel Trailhead ★

■ US Forest Service
▲ Ten-X (US Forest Service)
Summer camping only

TUSAYAN ■

64

To Valle, Williams, Flagstaff and Hwy 40

Grand Canyon Airport ■

♿ HOPI POINT ★

HERMITS REST ♿
Hermit Trailhead

Rim Trail

Hermit Trail

SOUTH RIM

◈ Tower of Ra

GORGE

◈ Diana Temple

N

0   5 mi

0   5 km

What Makes the South Rim of the Grand Canyon Special

- Hiking in one of the most amazing natural wonders on the planet

- Knowing that if you make it the canyon floor, you are amongst rock that is 2.2 billion years old, some of the oldest exposed rock on earth

- The grandeur of the mesas, the magnitude of the various rock layers, the sheer immensity, it's the Grand Canyon!

Hiking in the South Rim of the Grand Canyon

Rim Trail

Easy – (13.0 mi / 21.0 km), one way, time varies on route taken, elev. Δ: 200 ft / 61m, trailhead at viewpoint at Grand Canyon Village and along Hermit Road

The Rim Trail is great for just strolling in the Grand Canyon with the view slowly changing before you. The trail starts at the South Kaibab Trailhead and extends to Hermit's Rest. It can be picked up from any overlook, and by utilizing the shuttle system one can pick up the trail and drop off it with a great deal of convenience. The trail is mostly paved and well traveled. For quieter moments, try walking it in tune to the sunrise or meander along its route in the late afternoon into dusk.

Bright Angel Trail

Strenuous – (12.0 mi / 19.3 km to Plateau Point), round trip, allow 5-8 hours, elev. Δ: 3,039 ft / 926 m, trailhead west of Bright Angel Lodge

Strenuous – (17.6 mi / 28.3 km to Colorado River), round trip, allow 5-8 hours, elev. Δ: 4,888 ft / 1,490 m, trailhead west of Bright Angel Lodge

Bright Angel is a very well defined trail that ultimately leads to the Colorado River itself. While it is possible to do this in one day, as mentioned above, this is an all-day hike and not for the casual hiker. The thing to realize about Bright Angel is it is very inviting and gives wonderful views as you immerse yourself into the depths of the canyon. However, the trail is steep, which gives you the impression

Panorama of the Grand Canyon

that you are "cooking with gas" as you travel downward. It is only on the return that you realize just how steep this trail is. Allow twice as much time for the return trip and bring twice as much water for this hot, exposed trail.

For groups with small children, going to the first switchback offers a good experience without subjecting little feet to the steeper bits just ahead. For those not looking to do a full 12-mile (19 km) hike, going to Indian Gardens offers great views and a nice stopping point before turning around. There is water to refill your canteen and even a ranger on duty most of the time. Indian Gardens is 9 miles (14.5 km) round trip. If you decide to go the 1.5 miles (2.4 km) farther to Plateau Point, you won't be disappointed. This fairly level trail takes you to a nice viewpoint of the Colorado River and surrounding canyon. This is a great spot to get a good understanding of the immensity, grandeur, and beauty of the Grand Canyon. You'll see how far you've traveled, and upon looking at the river below, you'll see how far you would still need to go, which is humbling.

South Kaibab Trail

Strenuous – (6.0 mi / 9.7 km to Skeleton Point), round trip, allow 4 -5 hours, elev. Δ: 2,011 ft / 613 m, trailhead at Yaki Point off Desert View Drive

Strenuous – (12.0 mi / 19.3 km to Colorado River), round trip, allow 8 -10 hours, elev. Δ: 4,800 ft / 1,463 m,

From South Rim to Phantom Ranch: 6.9 mi / 11.1 km, to North Rim: 20.9 mi / 33.6 km

It is possible to take the South Kaibab Trail to the river and even connect over to Bright Angel, but most people do this as a multi-day trip due to the strenuous nature of the journey. Just like Bright Angel Trail, South Kaibab is steep, offers incredible views, and is very exposed. The first destination along the trail is Ooh-Aah Point, which offers an expansive view of the canyon and is less than 2 miles (3.2 km) round trip.

By the way, Ooh-Aah Point gets its name from an uncommon, nearly prehistoric language that is hotly debated by linguists as to its exact meaning. This is a rough translation, but most agree that "Ooh-Aah" means either

"Wow!" or "The-Place-of-Amazing-Self-ie-with-View-of-Grand-Canyon-About-One-Mile-From-Rim." You decide which translation works best for you.

There is a restroom at Cedar Ridge, but that is the extent of the facilities on the South Kaibab Trail. Cedar Ridge is about 1.5 miles (2.4 km) from the rim. Skeleton Point offers great views of the river and the surrounding area and is the recommended turnaround for day hikers.

On the question of South Kaibab versus Bright Angel, South Kaibab's fewer amenities means it is slightly less traveled than Bright Angel. That said there are very few hikers on these trails relative to the vast number of people looking over the canyon's edge at the rim. If you are looking to escape into your own personal experience of the canyon, either trail will get you there.

Hermit Trail

Strenuous – (17.8 mi / 28.6 km to Colorado River), round trip, allow 8-12 hours, elev. Δ: 4,340 ft / 1,323 m, trailhead at Hermits Rest

The Hermit Trail begins at Hermit's Rest and, like all the trails described here, is accessed via shuttle. This trail is great for many reasons if you are an experienced hiker looking for something a little more rugged. It was originally built by horse thieves during the nineteenth century and is today considered a threshold trail, which means the National Park doesn't actively maintain it. There is water to be found along the trail, but it needs to be treated. Some of the trail has rutted out in areas and, in some cases, rock slides covering the trail require one to do a little scrambling to navigate around them. The point here is, if you are an experienced hiker, the Hermit Trail offers just about everything, including an endpoint worthy of the journey. It is 8.9 miles (14 km) down to the river, but if

you are able to make it, you are rewarded with Hermit Rapids, perhaps the strongest hydraulics and biggest waves of any set of rapids in the canyon. The Hermit Rapids help to motivate any hiker and do not disappoint. You hear them before you see them and in seeing them there is nothing but gushing awe and respect.

It cannot be overstated that this is a trail to be taken seriously. Plan—bring the right gear, including plenty of food and water, and start early if you do plan to take on this all-day hike. There is a primitive campground at the river's edge and most folks do this as an overnight trip.

Grandview Trail

Strenuous – (6.0 mi / 9.7 km to Horseshoe Mesa / Toilet Junction), round trip, allow 4-5 hours, elev. Δ: 2,500 ft / 762 m, trailhead at Grandview Point along Desert View Drive

Grandview is one of the quickest ways to get down into the canyon. It is very steep in some places and during the winter is dangerously icy. Crampons or some other means of traction for your footwear is required in winter. The trail offers deep views into the canyon as well as ruins of historic mining structures. Another feature of the trail is the placement of log "cribs" in some of the vertical sections of the Kaibab/Toroweap section. Many of these log supports were swept away during a landslide in the winter of 2005, but there are a few examples of these historical trail structures still around.

From the bottom of the canyon

The Grandview Trail is not as well maintained as either Bright Angel or South Kaibab Trails. There are steep drop-offs in some areas. Use caution when hiking this trail.

River Rafting

Rafting down the Colorado is not only a popular activity, for many it is a bucket list item, something they have to do before they head on to the big national park in the sky. As a result, don't expect to show up and get on the river. Rafting is by permit only in the Grand Canyon and, depending on the activity, can take one to two years to receive a permit. The Park has made an effort to streamline the types of trips available and the permitting process for each.

That said, rafting down the Colorado through the Grand Canyon is truly a defining moment in anyone's life. It is an experience that moves beyond words, resets your definitions of awe and wonder, brings a restful peace to the soul and at times puts you in moments of unholy terror that—on getting to the other side of—help remind you just how awesome it is to be alive. It is worth the planning and the wait.

One Day Commercial River Trips:

Half day and full day smooth water river trips are available through park concessionaire Colorado River Discovery. You can purchase tickets at any of the park's lodges. The smooth water river trips are the only trips that do not require a permit and as the trip never encounters rapids, is open to all ages from four years old and up.

While these trips are gentle and without the excitement of white water, they are a great way to see the park and are highly recommended. Bring food and water, sunscreen, a hat and, of course, your camera. On a side note about the camera, yes, it's okay to bring a camera on the trip

that isn't waterproof as it is unlikely you will get wet. That said, use caution. In the summer, you won't need a towel as in the heat of the day you will dry off pretty quickly. In the spring and cooler seasons, bring layers. As you will be entering at the Glen Canyon Dam, which is inside the protection of Homeland Security, you will be checked for weapons, including pepper spray and pocket knives. These will not be allowed, so don't bring them.

Transportation from the lodge to the Dam is included.

3- to 18-Day Commercial River Trips

For those who are looking for white water rapids and adventure, there are hosts of river concessioners that provide full service guided trips. Each company offers its own suite of trips and many cater to the different experiences visitors are

A dory in Hance Rapids

looking for. Trips can last for as little as a few days to up to 18 days.

The upside of a guided trip is that, first and foremost, you don't need to become an expert in white water rafting. The domain of the rafter is a world unto itself. They have their own language, and while they are a friendly, tightly knitted group, it's an investment of time and money to enter their world and walk, err—paddle—among them. A guided trip comes with the security that you are riding down the Colorado with an expert at the helm. Plus, the thoughts of where to camp, what to eat, and even where to do your business are pretty much taken care of for you. The downside is the cost and the fact that reservations need to be made one to two years in advance.

Details on what trips are offered, in what type of raft, duration and other amenities are numerous. The best place to start is the Grand Canyon NPS page, which lists all of the river concessionaires. Go to: http://www.nps.gov/grca/planyourvisit/river-concessioners.htm

2- to 5-Day Noncommercial River Trips

Permits are available to the general public starting one year in advance and are assigned on a first come, first served basis. Two noncommercial permits are authorized each day launching from Diamond Creek. Each trip is limited to a maximum of 16 people. There is no fee for the permits and they can be obtained by filling out a permit application and mailing it to the NPS permits department. While the NPS does not charge a fee for the permit, the Hualapai Tribe does charge a fee for crossing their land.

The permit can be found by going to: http://www.nps.gov/grca/planyourvisit/upload/Diamond_Creek_Application. pdfYou can also call directly: (800) 959-9164 or (928) 638-7843.

As mentioned above, you are crossing both National Park Service land and Hualapai tribal land. Hualapai means "people of the tall trees" in reference to the Ponderosa Pine. This small community of about 2,000 individuals primarily bases its economy on tourism. One way they do that is to charge a fee for each person (including drivers) and each vehicle traveling Diamond Creek Road, which they own. Cost is $64.20 for each person and vehicle, (example: 16 passengers, 2 drivers and 2 vehicles will cost $1284 total). Camping on the south side of the river (river left) above the high water mark will also require a permit from the Haulapai. More information can be had by calling the Haulapai directly at (928) 769-2219.

The NPS permits authorize you and your group to travel for 2 to 5 days from Diamond Creek in the Lower Gorge of the Colorado River. This 52-mile (84 km) section is spectacular and includes both

smooth water and some decent rapids to shoot as well as culturally significant areas. River users are asked to treat these cultural areas with respect so that future generations can enjoy them. Camping is limited but is free on the north side (river right).

One word of note: acceptance. The river has changed since the days of Powell. You will be sharing the river with many other users, especially at the launch and take-out areas. You will find motorized upstream and downstream travel from Lake Mead and even see a helicopter or two. There will be moments that are all yours, but there will also be moments that are shared with others

12- to 25-Day Noncommercial River Trips

This type of self-guided river trip travels among the rugged section between Lees Ferry to Diamond Creek and is for those fully experienced in river rafting. The permits are made available through a weighted lottery. For more information, start here: http://www.nps.gov/grca/planyourvisit/overview-lees-ferry-dia-mond-ck.htm.

Mule Trips

The mule rides offered by park concessionaire Xanterra are a classic way of seeing the Grand Canyon. The day trips offered change seasonally, and new offerings open up at the whim of the concessionaire. Most rides are typically 3-hour, 4-mile (6.4 km) rides. You don't need prior experience riding a mule, and your tour will include a fair amount of interesting interpretation about the geology and human history along the trail.

Overnight tours are also offered, and this ride is on par with rafting down the Colorado River in terms of generating incredible memories. You will ride your mule to Phantom Ranch located near the river. Lunch is provided and the steak dinner at the ranch is hearty and very welcome after the day's journey. As with the day trips, the overnight trips are full of interpretive narration on nearly all aspects of the park. The overnight trip to Phantom Ranch has been a high water mark for many visitors.

The downsides to the mule trips are the expense and the fact that you need to reserve the event well in advance. There

Grand Canyon with clouds overhead

is a wait list for day-before cancellations; however, the chances of people canceling are very slim. As of June 2014, it cost $548.84 for one person or $960.01 for two to ride a mule to Phantom Ranch and spend the night there.

Mule rides from the South Rim can be reserved through:

Xanterra Parks & Resorts (303) 297-2757, (888) 297-2757

Virtual Caching

For those who have never heard of this, virtual caching is the delightful marriage of treasure hunting and technology. Specifically, a "cache" is a term that denotes a bunch of stuff stowed somewhere in the wilderness. With virtual caching, a visitor uses his or her GPS system to find the cache. The reward is in part the journey and in part finding the cache, which— being virtual—means what you find is a cool location.

The National Park Service has done a wonderful job of offering an interesting way to explore the park.

You will need a GPS device (or smart phone with GPS), the park map, which is located inside the park's official newspaper, The Guide, and a copy of the instruction sheet, titled "Story of Grand Canyon." The instructions can be picked up at the Grand Canyon Visitor Center, where different coordinates are listed. Input the coordinates into your GPS device and take the shuttle or walk to the various destinations. None of the virtual caching is done off trail; everything can be found on the paved rim of the park and on the trails. Along the way, the instruction sheet acts as an educational pamphlet on different aspects of the park. Virtual caching is a cool way to discover new things about the park, and if you are navigationally challenged, perhaps a way of discovering a bit about yourself as well!

You will need to keep a record of all your coordinates, which will be necessary to solve the final clue. It takes about 4–6 hours to complete this puzzle, and the tour will take you over a good deal of the park along the way. You can, in the end, receive a certificate of completion. See the visitor center for more details.

Driving Around

Like Zion NP and Bryce NP, Grand Canyon receives too many visitors to make driving around the park practical. The NPS offers a fairly robust shuttle system to get you around, and it is not only highly recommended to use the shuttle system; it is the only method year round for some roads and during peak season for others.

In general, the shuttle system is divided into two loops, the Village Route and Kaibab Rim Route. The Village Route goes to the west and stops at Mather Campground, Trailer Village, Market Plaza, Grand Canyon Visitor Center, Shrine of the Ages, Train Depot, Bright Angel Lodge and Trailhead, and Maswik Lodge. The Village Route also stops at the

Desert View Watchtower

Hermit's Rest Transfer, which is where you pick up the Hermit's Rest shuttle during peak season.

The Kaibab Route winds to the east and stops at the Grand Canyon Visitor Center, South Kaibab Trailhead, Yaki Point, Pipe Creek Vista, Mather Point and Yavapai Geology Museum.

You can drive on Hermit's Rest Road during the winter months and, to the east, the Desert View is a wonderful drive that ultimately takes you to the East Rim of the Grand Canyon.

There is so much to do in the South Rim of the Grand Canyon

There is a tremendous number of things to do and see, more than this little all-inclusive guidebook of seven National Parks can manage to describe in detail. Here are a few places worth exploring further:

Kolb Studio

Art gallery, photo gallery, bookstore and place of historical interest run by the Grand Canyon Association. Near the Bright Angel Lodge

El Tovar Hotel

Built in 1905, this hotel is on the National Register of Historic Places. It is noted for its Arts and Crafts as well as Mission style interior and exterior and is an incredible example of early twentieth century National Park lodge architecture.

Yavapai Geology Museum

A great place to learn everything you wanted to know about the geology of the Grand Canyon. Many exhibits, three dimensional models and photographs along with the outdoor nature and geology "Trail of Time" where each meter traveled on the trail represents one

million years of the geology of the Grand Canyon. If you think about it, the "Trail of Time" took about 2 billion years to make, so it is well worth seeing.

Desert View Watchtower

Located on the East Rim of the park, the four story, 70-foot-high (21m) stone building was built in 1932 by Fred Harvey Architect Mary Colter. Mary Colter designed many of the buildings in the Grand Canyon, including Hopi House, Lookout Studio, Bright Angel Lodge, the Phantom Ranch buildings and Hermit's Rest (but not El Tovar Lodge). Patterned after the Pueblo kivas and watchtowers, the watchtower has a unique touch in its design.

Skywalk

The Skywalk is managed by the Hualapai Tribe and is located on their tribal lands. It is a horseshoe-shaped walkway securely bolted into the canyon walls such that is juts out over the canyon itself. With the floors and sides made of glass, the structure juts out about 70 feet (21m) from the canyon rim, giving the feeling that you are suspended in air over the canyon. It is one of the most famous attractions within the western portion of the Grand Canyon. There is a separate fee for this attraction. Skywalk reservations: 1-888-868-9378 or 1-928-769-2636

Skywalk

Grand Canyon National Park - North Rim

Quick Facts

Official Park Website: http://www.nps.gov/grca

Visitor Center:

- General Visitor Information: (928) 638-7888

- Backcountry Information Center: (928) 638-7875

View from the North Rim

Park Accessibility:

- Okay for 2WD and RVs

- Day and Overnight Use (seasonally)

Experience Level:
- Family Friendly – Backcountry Hiker

Camping in Park:
Reservations strongly recommended at (877) 444-6777 or online at the http://www.recreation.gov/
- North Rim Campground: 90 T/RV, seasonal (closed in winter), drinking water, flush toilets, pull-thru sites, no hookups, dump station, group sites available.

Lodging in Park:
- North Rim Lodge, closed in winter. Reservations strongly recommended at (877) 386-4383.

Dining in Park:
- Multiple dining options and market at North Rim Lodge, closed in winter.

Nearest Town with Amenities:
- Jacob Lake, AZ is 44 mi / 71 km from park

Getting There:
- From St George, UT: take I-15 North to UT-59 South to AZ-389 East, turn right onto US-89A South to AZ-67 South to North Rim park entrance

What Makes the North Rim of the Grand Canyon Special

- The less crowded, more intimate side of the Grand Canyon

- For those that have done the South Rim, knowing you are about to hike new trails within one of the most scenic places on earth

- The better side to start a "rim to rim" day hike because the longer of the two sides is downhill if you come from the North Rim

Granted the North Rim is a bit harder to get to and is closed during the winter season, but the reward is far fewer people. It brings the ability to see the Grand Canyon more on your terms and pace, receiving around 500,000 visitors annually. The North Rim is higher in elevation and thus can be cooler. This side of the canyon is up to 1800 feet higher, making day trips down to the river and back longer than the South Rim.

Hiking the North Rim of the Grand Canyon

Bright Angel Point Trail

Easy – (0.5 mi / 0.8 km), round trip, allow 30 minutes, elev. Δ: 200 ft / 61m, trailhead near visitor center

Bright Angel Point is a nice walk from Grand Canyon Lodge and nearby visitor center. There are examples of marine fossils within the rocks along the way. Be sure to pick a park brochure, which shows the location of the fossils and gives a good historical backstory of the lodge and this historic trail.

Transept Trail

Easy – (3.0 mi / 4.8 km), round trip, allow 1 - 2 hours, elev. Δ: 150 ft / 46 m, trailhead near North Rim Lodge

The Transept Trail starts at the Grand Canyon Lodge and follows the rim of the canyon to the North Rim Campground. Great views along the way.

North Rim with cloud play

Ken Patrick Trail

Strenuous – (10.0 mi / 16.0 km), one way, 5 - 6 hours, elev. Δ: 600 ft / 183 m, trailhead north of visitor center at North Kaibab trailhead

The Ken Patrick Trail is named after a ranger killed in the line of duty. He is buried within the Grand Canyon, but worked at Point Reyes National Seashore and was killed by poachers in 1973.

This there and back trail is best accomplished with two cars. Starting from the North Kaibab Trailhead, the Ken Patrick Trail starts off clearly for the first 2 ½ miles but can become very difficult to find after reaching the Old Bright Angel Trail sign post. If you are an experienced hiker and this sounds appealing, simply keep north and don't go too far from the rim. Once you pick up the Cape Royal Road, the trail becomes easier to find and maintains close to the rim all the way to Point Imperial.

Lower Ribbon Falls

Uncle Jim Trail

Moderate – (5.0 mi / 8.0 km), round trip, allow 2 - 3 hours, elev. Δ: 100 ft / 30 m, trailhead north of visitor center at North Kaibab trailhead

This trail starts from the same parking lot as the North Kaibab Trailhead and meanders through the Kaibab Plateau forest to Uncle Jim's Point, which overlooks Bright Angel, Roaring Springs and an overall spectacular view of the canyon.

Bridle Trail

Easy – (1.2 mi / 2.0 km), one way, allow 1 hour, elev. Δ: 161 ft / 49m, trailheads at viewpoint at North Rim Lodge and at North Kaibab Trailhead

A gentle trail that parallels the road from the Grand Canyon Lodge to the North Kaibab Trailhead. The Bridle Trail is a great after dinner hike to take in the peace of the canyon.

North Kaibab Trail

Strenuous – (14.0 mi / 22.5 km), one way, allow 6-10 hours, elev. Δ: 5,780 ft / 1,762 m, trailhead north of visitor center at North Kaibab trailhead

Note that while the total distance to the river is shown, it does not include the distance back. This is because the total distance to the Colorado River and back is 28 miles and is definitely not recommended as a day hike. Folks do use the North Kaibab Trail as the starting point for a rim-to-rim hike, primarily because the trip for the longer leg of the two sides is downhill if you start on from the North Rim.

The North Kaibab Trail is special because it is starts at a higher elevation than either South Kaibab or Bright Angel trails. The 1,000-foot increase in elevation is such that a hike down the North Kaibab Trail to the Colorado River means you will pass through every ecosystem found between Canada and Mexico. It is the least visited of the maintained trails and is also the most strenuous. It is definitely a serious day hike at 28 miles (45 km) round trip and is typically done as a backpacking trip. There are a few restroom facilities and seasonal water available, though the water will need to be treated.

The trail heads steeply down at first until it flattens out a bit as you enter into the base of Bright Angel Canyon. At 5.0 miles (8.0 km), you encounter Roaring Springs, which is a short side trip that is easily visible from the trail. Here you can see water coming directly out of the cliff, typically with a nice flow, creating a little island of moss and ferns within the desert. Roaring Springs flows into Bright Angel Creek as you continue down the trail. This is an important water source, delivering the drinking water for every visitor within Grand Canyon NP. If you make it to the Colorado River, you can see the pipe going over the river on the underside of Bright Angel Trail's Silver Bridge.

Just a little farther down at 5.4 miles (8.7 km) is a structure known as the Pumphouse Residence, or Aiken Residence. From 1973 to 2006, Bruce Aiken was an artist, NP employee, and pump mas-ter, overseeing the water supply for the park. He and his wife Mary raised three children at the canyon bottom and lucky hikers were greeted with lemonade from the children from time to time. Aiken's work reflects a fine-tuned harmony with the area of the Grand Canyon. Working mainly in oil, the light, balance, and overall portrayal of rock and water are testimonies to living within the Grand Canyon, raising a family and experiencing nearly each day of one's life for 33 years inside its walls.

Another treasure on the North Kaibab is Ribbon Falls at 8.5 miles (13.7 km). It is a little grotto in the desert cascading gently on the west side of Bright Angel Creek. It is a great place to get out of the heat of the day, which can be intense in the summer. Between the Cottonwood Campground and Bright Angel Campground, you enter the Inner Gorge, which is a narrow canyon of the 2 billion-year-old Vishnu Schist. If you make it this far, you are now walking among rock roughly half as old as the earth itself. You can connect to either the South Kaibab or Bright Angel Trail over the two bridges that cross the Colorado at the canyon bottom.

South of Point Imperial

At this point you may be thinking North Kaibab is a gem of a trail, (which it is), and thus wondering if you could do a rim-to-rim adventure. The good news is you can. Trans Canyon Shuttle offers two rim-to-rim shuttles daily (go to http://www.trans-canyonshuttle.com for more info). The not-so-good news is getting reservations at one of the primitive campgrounds is a challenge. In addition, the shuttles depart early morning and early afternoon, so factor in an overnight stay at the opposing rim or hoofing it out to make the shuttle on the last day.

Widforss Trail

Strenuous – (10.0 mi / 16.0 km), round trip allow 4 – 5 hours, elev. Δ: 400 ft / 122 m, trailhead north of visitor center west of North Kaibab trailhead

The Widforss Trail may just be the longest interpretive trail in the entire Grand Circle. Be sure to pick up a brochure at the trailhead. The trail hugs the canyon rim for the first half of the hike and then heads into a forested area to end at Widforss Point. The expansiveness of the Grand Canyon from this vista is impressive and it was a favorite of Gunnar Widforss, an early twentieth century landscape artist.

Arizona Trail

Strenuous – (12.6 mi / 20.3 km), one way, allow 5 - 6 hours, trailheads at North Kaibab trailhead and Kaibab National Forest boundary

The Arizona Trail is an 800-mile adventure that starts in Mexico and heads northward until it ends in Utah. A part of the trail leverages the existing north and south rim to rim trails of Grand Canyon NP. From the North Kaibab Trail, it continues through the park for another 10 miles before hitting the park's boundary. This portion roughly follows Highway 67, traveling through forest canopy and the Harvey Meadow.

Point Imperial Trail

Easy – (4.0 mi / 6.4 km), round trip, allow 1.5 - 2 hours, elev. Δ: negligible, trailhead at end of Point Imperial Road

This is an easy hike through an area recovering from a wildfire in 2000 and is great way to take in the tenacity of nature recovering from devastation. On the way, one will see young Aspens and innocent wildflowers starting anew from the aftermath of the fire. This is a great hike for a sunrise at Point Imperial.

Roosevelt Point Trail

Easy – (0.2 mi / 0.3 km), round trip, allow 30 minutes, elev. Δ: negligible, trailhead at Cape Royal Road

More of a pleasant walk than a hike, this little ditty leads to a nice bench with great views of the canyon.

Cape Final Trail

Easy – (4.0 mi / 6.4 km), round trip, allow 1.5 - 2 hours, elev. Δ: 150 ft / 46 m, trailhead at Cape Royal Road

An easy trail that ends at one of the higher elevation views of the Grand Canyon at Cape Final. As this trail is not often used, it provides good promise if you are looking for a secluded and peaceful hike. Cape Final is at 7,850 feet. Be careful if you decide to go onto the ledge's edge, it's a long way down.

Cliff Springs Trail

Easy – (1.0 mi / 1.6 km), round trip, allow 45 – 60 minutes, elev. Δ: 150 ft / 46 m, trailhead at end of Cape Royal Road

A refreshing hike through a wooded ravine to a rocky overhang containing a seeping spring. The water is not suitable for drinking directly as tempting as it may seem. The spring holds an ecosystem for ferns and moss and can provide some nice shade from the day's sun. Look for the remains of a granary from the original inhabitants of the area early into the hike.

Cape Royal Trail

Easy – (0.6 mi / 1.0 km), round trip, allow 30 minutes, elev. Δ: 40 ft / 12 m, trailhead at end of Cape Royal Road

An easy, flat walk that allows views of Angels Window arch, the Colorado River, and if you look through the arch at the right angle, you can see both at the same time! Great photo opportunity and easy to access. There are interpretative markers along the way.

Ewe in the canyon

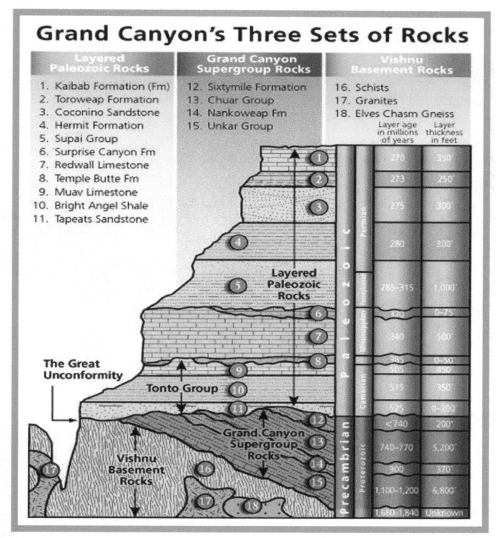

Grand Canyon's Three Sets of Rocks

Layered Paleozoic Rocks	Grand Canyon Supergroup Rocks	Vishnu Basement Rocks
1. Kaibab Formation (Fm)	12. Sixtymile Formation	16. Schists
2. Toroweap Formation	13. Chuar Group	17. Granites
3. Coconino Sandstone	14. Nankoweap Fm	18. Elves Chasm Gneiss
4. Hermit Formation	15. Unkar Group	
5. Supai Group		
6. Surprise Canyon Fm		
7. Redwall Limestone		
8. Temple Butte Fm		
9. Muav Limestone		
10. Bright Angel Shale		
11. Tapeats Sandstone		

Layered Paleozoic Rocks

The Great Unconformity

Tonto Group

Grand Canyon Supergroup Rocks

Vishnu Basement Rocks

	Layer age in millions of years	Layer thickness in feet
1	270	350'
2	273	250'
3	275	300'
4	280	300'
5	285–315	1,000'
6	320	0–75'
7	340	500'
8	385	0–50'
9	505	450'
10	515	350'
11	525	0–200'
12	<740	200'
13	740–770	5,200'
14	900	370'
15	1,100–1,200	6,800'
	1,580–1,840	Unknown

The geology of the Grand Canyon

Pipe Spring National Monument

Official Park Website: http://www.nps.gov/pisp

Visitor Center:

- (928) 643-7105

Park Accessibility:

- Okay for 2WD and RVs
- Day Use Only

Experience Level:

- Family Friendly

Camping in Park:

- None

Lodging and Dining in Park:

- None

Nearest Town with Amenities:

- Fredonia, AZ is 14 mi / 23 km from the park

Getting There:

- From St. George, UT: take UT-59 South and AZ-389 East for 60 mi / 97 km to the park

Covered wagon at Pipe Spring National Monument

What Makes Pipe Spring National Monument Special

- Touring a remote 19th century Mormon fortified ranch house in Arizona

- Learning about a period when your greatest fears were getting raided by the Navajo

- Checking out one of the best museums and visitor centers in the Grand Circle

Pipe Spring was first discovered in 1858 by Jacob Hamblin, a Mormon missionary on an expedition to the Hopi mesas. Two years later, James M. Whitmore and a group of fellow pioneers created a homestead and cattle operation. Building a group of homes in Navajo territory was one thing, keeping it was another. Once the Apache, Navajo, Utes, and Paiutes joined forces to start the Black Hawk War in 1866, primarily aimed at the Mormons, things came to a boiling point. After a raid of the Pipe Springs homesteads, it was decided to build a fort over the main spring.

This fortified ranch house was purchased by Brigham Young in 1872 for the Church of the Latter Day Saints (LDS). Brigham sent Mormon Bishop Anson Perry Winsor to run the ranch and he renamed it Winsor Castle. The ranch became a safe haven for travelers passing through and even acted as a refuge for polygamist wives during the late 1800's. In the end, the ranch's ties to polygamy would be its downfall and the LDS lost ownership of the property in 1887.

Today the monument is a cultural preserve, offering a 30-minute ranger led tour of the ranch house and an extensive museum and visitor center. It is also possible to take a self-guided walk amongst the out buildings, corral, and garden areas. Pipe Spring National Monument offers an informative and interesting step back in time; especially if the ranger led tour is taken. Definitely worth the drive.

Pipe Spring

The historic Winsor Castle

Southwest Utah

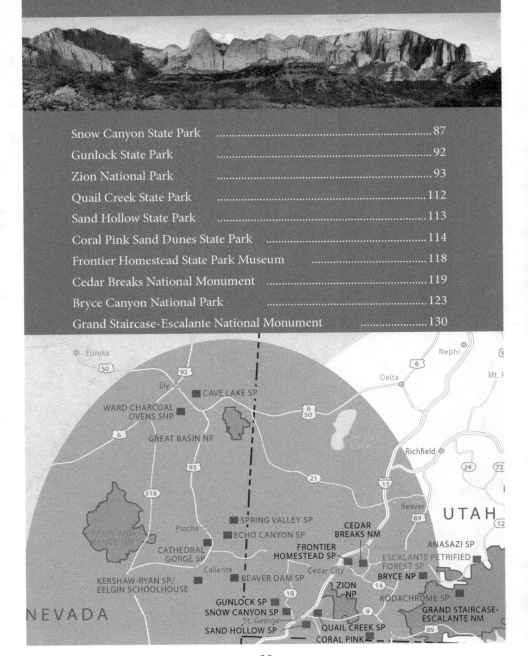

Eureka

Nephi

Ely

CAVE LAKE SP

Delta

Mt. F

WARD CHARCOAL
OVENS SHP

GREAT BASIN NP

Richfield

SPRING VALLEY SP

CEDAR
BREAKS NM

UTAH

ECHO CANYON SP

ANASAZI SP

Pioche

FRONTIER
HOMESTEAD SP

ESCALANTE PETRIFIED
FOREST SP

BASIN AND
RANGE NM

CATHEDRAL
GORGE SP

Caliente

Cedar City

BRYCE NP

KERSHAW-RYAN SP/
EELGIN SCHOOLHOUSE

BEAVER DAM SP

ZION
NP

KODACHROME SP

NEVADA

GUNLOCK SP

SNOW CANYON SP

St. George

GRAND STAIRCASE-
ESCALANTE NM

SAND HOLLOW SP

QUAIL CREEK SP

CORAL PINK

Snow Canyon State Park

Quick Facts

Official Park Website: http://stateparks.utah.gov/parks/snow-canyon/

Visitor Center: (435) 628-2255

Park Accessibility:
- Okay for 2WD and RVs
- Day and Overnight Use

Experience Level:
- Family Friendly to Experienced Hiker

Camping in Park:
- Snow Canyon Campground: 31 T/RV, drinking water, flush toilets, showers, hookups, dump station, some pull thru sites, call visitor center for reservations

Lodging and Dining in Park:
- None

Nearest Town with Amenities:
- Ivins, UT is 4 mi / 6 km from park

Getting There:
- From St George, UT: Take UT-18 North to Snow Canyon Drive. Total distance is 13 mi / 21 km to park

Sweeping views and fantastic trails at Snow Canyon State Park

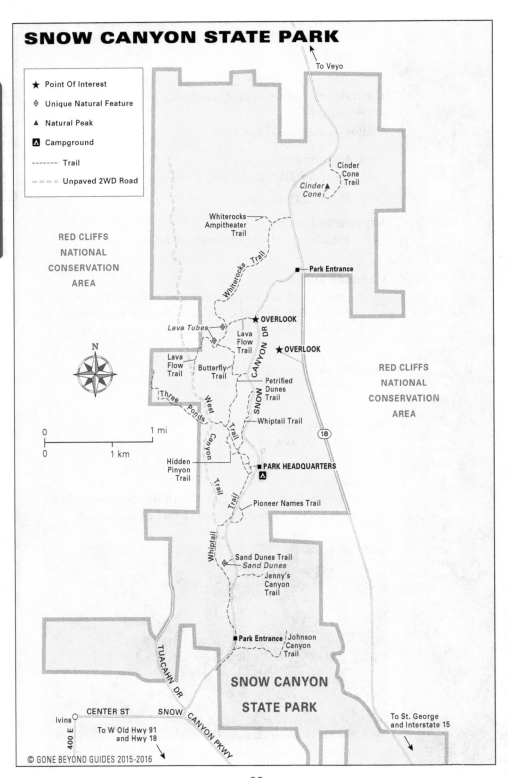

SNOW CANYON STATE PARK

SOUTHWEST UTAH

Snow Canyon

Legend:
- ★ Point Of Interest
- ◇ Unique Natural Feature
- ▲ Natural Peak
- 🅰 Campground
- -------- Trail
- ==== Unpaved 2WD Road

To Veyo

Cinder Cone Trail

Cinder Cone ▲

Whiterocks Ampitheater Trail

Whiterocks Trail

Park Entrance

RED CLIFFS NATIONAL CONSERVATION AREA

★ OVERLOOK

Lava Tubes ◇

Lava Flow Trail

★ OVERLOOK

RED CLIFFS NATIONAL CONSERVATION AREA

Lava Flow Trail

Butterfly Trail

SNOW CANYON DR

Three Ponds

West Canyon Trail

Petrified Dunes Trail

Whiptail Trail

(18)

N

0 ————— 1 mi
0 ————— 1 km

Hidden Pinyon Trail

Whiptail Trail

■ PARK HEADQUARTERS 🅰

Pioneer Names Trail

Sand Dunes Trail
Sand Dunes ◇

Jenny's Canyon Trail

■ Park Entrance | Johnson Canyon Trail

SNOW CANYON STATE PARK

TUACAHN DR

CENTER ST   SNOW

Ivins

400 E

To W Old Hwy 91 and Hwy 18

SNOW CANYON PKWY

To St. George and Interstate 15

© GONE BEYOND GUIDES 2015-2016

What Makes Snow Canyon State Park Special

- One of the few places in the Grand Circle where Navajo sandstone and lava have mixed
- Some incredible slick rock exploration
- Remarkably close to civilization and yet remote at the same time

Snow Canyon State Park has some amazing views, even as you pull up. From a distance, the broad panorama of red and white sandstone, with a hint of lava-capped adventure in the background, is simply breathtaking. One's eye, just on the approach, can gaze merrily for hours, sweeping back and forth along the lines of white to red sandstone. It is, even on the horizon, a place of sandstone as art.

This natural display is only intensified as one draws in and onto the trail. There are sand dunes, hoodoos, fins, razor thin labyrinths, and canyons that beckon with their twists and turns to hike around just one more bend. The rock is bright with color and the possibilities for hiking seem endless. There are petroglyphs and other evidence of use prior to modern times as well.

Snow Canyon is a place of slickrock magic to be sure, but there is more to the park than just carved sandstone. There is also a section where lava has covered over, creating a different exploration. Within this area are lava tubes, caves, and lava flows with some cool features to discover. In fact, the park's tallest feature is a cinder cone.

Snow Canyon offers camping and a lot of established trails. Given that it's close to St. George and Ivins, Utah makes this a great day hiking spot for travelers that don't want to camp.

Hiking Snow Canyon State Park

Johnson Canyon

Easy – (2.0 mi / 3.2 km), round trip, allow 1 hour

This trail is closed from March 15 to October 31 to protect nesting bird populations. When open, this is considered one of the top hikes in the park. Easy and level, the trail passes by a natural spring and ends at a monster thick arch spanning 200 feet.

Whiptail Trail

Easy – (6.0 mi / 9.7 km), round trip, allow 3 hours

Whiptail is a paved there and back route popular with the locals. There are plenty of bikers, joggers, and walkers on this trail. The trail sits at the base of Snow Canyon's red (and white) rocks, giving a nice backdrop for all users. There is a small elevation gain but the trail is wheelchair accessible. This is a popular hike, especially on weekends.

Jenny's Canyon

Easy – (0.5 mi / 0.8 km), round trip, allow 30 minutes

This trail is closed from March 15 to June 1 to protect nesting bird populations. A short level hike that ends at an interesting slot canyon. Jenny's Canyon Trail is great for kids.

Sand Dunes

Easy – (0.5 mi / 0.8 km), round trip, allow 30 minutes

A quick an easy jaunt to a small set of sand dunes. This is a great family hike with fabulous scenery from every angle. If you have small children, this is a perfect place for playing in the dunes.

Pioneer Names Trail

Easy – (0.5 mi / 0.8 km), round trip, allow 30 minutes

Pioneer Names Trail takes a somewhat sandy but otherwise ambling and quick path to a red rock alcove. Within it are the names of several Mormon pioneers from 1881. Getting to the alcove and up close to the pioneer graffiti requires a short but steep climb up slick rock at the end. The surroundings are a pleasing mix of red sandstone and the green of the desert pinyon juniper woodlands.

West Canyon Trail

Moderate – (8.0 mi / 12.9 km), round trip, allow 4 hours

This trail is an old dirt road that leads up into the main canyon in the park. The hike itself is level for the most part and offers great views into all of the side washes, sand stone hills, and cliff faces. This is a great place to go on an adventure, with plenty of slickrock to explore. The canyon is wide and inviting, traveling much of the time through grasslands. Stay on the trail whenever possible and avoid walking on undisturbed soil.

Hidden Pinyon

Moderate – (1.5 mi / 2.4 km), round trip, allow 1 hour

Stunning views are to be found on this hike. Great hike to capture the essence of the park in a short amount of time. This is an interpretive trail that describes the geologic features and native flora in the park.

Three Ponds

Moderate – (3.5 mi / 5.6 km), round trip, allow 2 hours

This is for the most part a hike through a sandy wash with some slick rock. The trail follows through a twisty wash with deep "slog worthy" sand to the mouth of a large canyon. The trail ends at the first of three potholes that seasonally fill with water. There are two other pools further on. While hiking to murky stagnant water may not be for everyone, the surroundings along the way are very nice and sure to please.

Petrified Dunes Trail

Moderate – (1.0 mi / 1.6 km), round trip, allow 45 minutes

Here is another trail taking the hiker to "sand dunes frozen in time". Geologically speaking, much of the Grand Circle

was a vast sand dune, so in effect, all the redrock you see falls under this moniker. That said, this is one of the nicest hikes in the park. The sandstone here is unique, odd, and beautiful, all at the same time.

Butterfly Trail

Moderate – (2.0 mi / 3.2 km), round trip, allow 1 hour

This trail is a continuation of Petrified Dunes Trail giving similar awesome scenery. Connects with West Canyon Overlook and the Lava Flow Trail. Some steep sections.

Lava Flow Trail

Moderate – (2.5 mi / 4.0 km), round trip, allow 1 - 2 hours

This is an easy to follow trail with some caves near the trailhead. Bring your headlamps. The trail itself is uneven throughout as it heads up into an ancient lava field. This trail can be very hot in the summer, but does show a different side of the park.

Whiterocks Amphitheater

Moderate – (4.0 mi / 6.4 km), round trip, allow 2 hours

This is a straightforward trail into the main white sandstone area of Snow Canyon. The trail starts out in moderately deep sand, but quickly hits the slickrock for an ascent of about 100 feet. The trail officially ends at a bowl of white rock, surrounding the hiker in amphitheater fashion, on three sides. It is possible to continue on in scramble mode to the top for better views. Some parts require Class 3 level scrambling. At the top, the hiker is rewarded with some fantastic views of the park.

There is a shorter trail of about one mile in length located north of the junction of Snow Canyon Drive and SR18 (north of the junction 0.5 miles).

Cinder Cone Trail

Strenuous – (1.5 mi / 2.4 km), round trip, allow 1 - 2 hours

Hiking up cinder cones can feel like you are going nowhere fast, but the trail does reach the top. The trail corkscrews up with an elevation gain of 500 feet. Once at the top, you will be greeted with a view of the crater and the park's gorgeous views.

Snow Canyon

Gunlock State Park

The Picturesque Waterfalls at Gunlock State Park

Official Park Website: http://stateparks.utah.gov/parks/gunlock//

Visitor Center: (435) 680-0715

Park Accessibility:
- Okay for 2WD and RVs
- Day and Overnight Use

Camping in Park:
- Gunlock Campground: 5 T/RV, no water, vault toilets, first come-first served

Getting There:
- From St George, UT: Take Old US Hwy 91 East. Total distance is 20 mi / 32 km to park

What Makes Gunlock State Park Special

- A very unique and fun set of waterfalls and pools to play in
- Boating and fishing, but read below
- Close to St. George, Utah

Although Sand Hollow is very close to Quail Creek State Park and despite both Gunlock is a small 266-acre park that protects a reservoir of the same name. The park is mainly a day use area for boating and fishing, though there is a campground for overnighters.

One of the nicest part of Gunlock Park is a beautiful set of waterfalls at the south end of the park. Referred to as the Gunlock Falls and Pools, this area of cascading waterfalls over angled and red slickrock is a favorite amongst locals.

Recently, the park has closed for day use due to the drought. As of this writing, the park is open through September. Check the website before going to see current conditions. They do update the water level stats frequently.

Zion National Park

Quick Facts

Official Park Website: www.nps.gov/zion

Visitor Center:

(435) 772-3256

Park Accessibility:

- Okay for 2WD and RVs
- Day and Overnight Use

Experience Level:

- Family Friendly to Experienced Hiker

Within The Narrows

Camping in Park:

- Watchman: 176 T/RV, 2 ADA, 6 group sites, host on site, water, hookups, reservations at www.recreation.gov or by calling (877) 444-6777
- South: 127 T/RV, 3 ADA, host on site, water, no hookups, first come/first served, open seasonally
- Lava Point: 6T, Pit Toilets, no water, first come/first served, open seasonally

Lodging in Park:

- Zion Lodge: (888) 297-2757

Dining in Park:

There are two options, both at Zion Lodge

- Red Rock Grill Dining Room, open year round, reservations recommended, (435) 772-3213
- Castle Dome Café, open seasonally

Nearest Town with Amenities:

- Springdale, Utah is within 1 mi / 2 km of main park entrance

Getting There:

- From St George, UT: Take I-15 North to UT-9 East. Total distance is 41 mi / 66 km to park

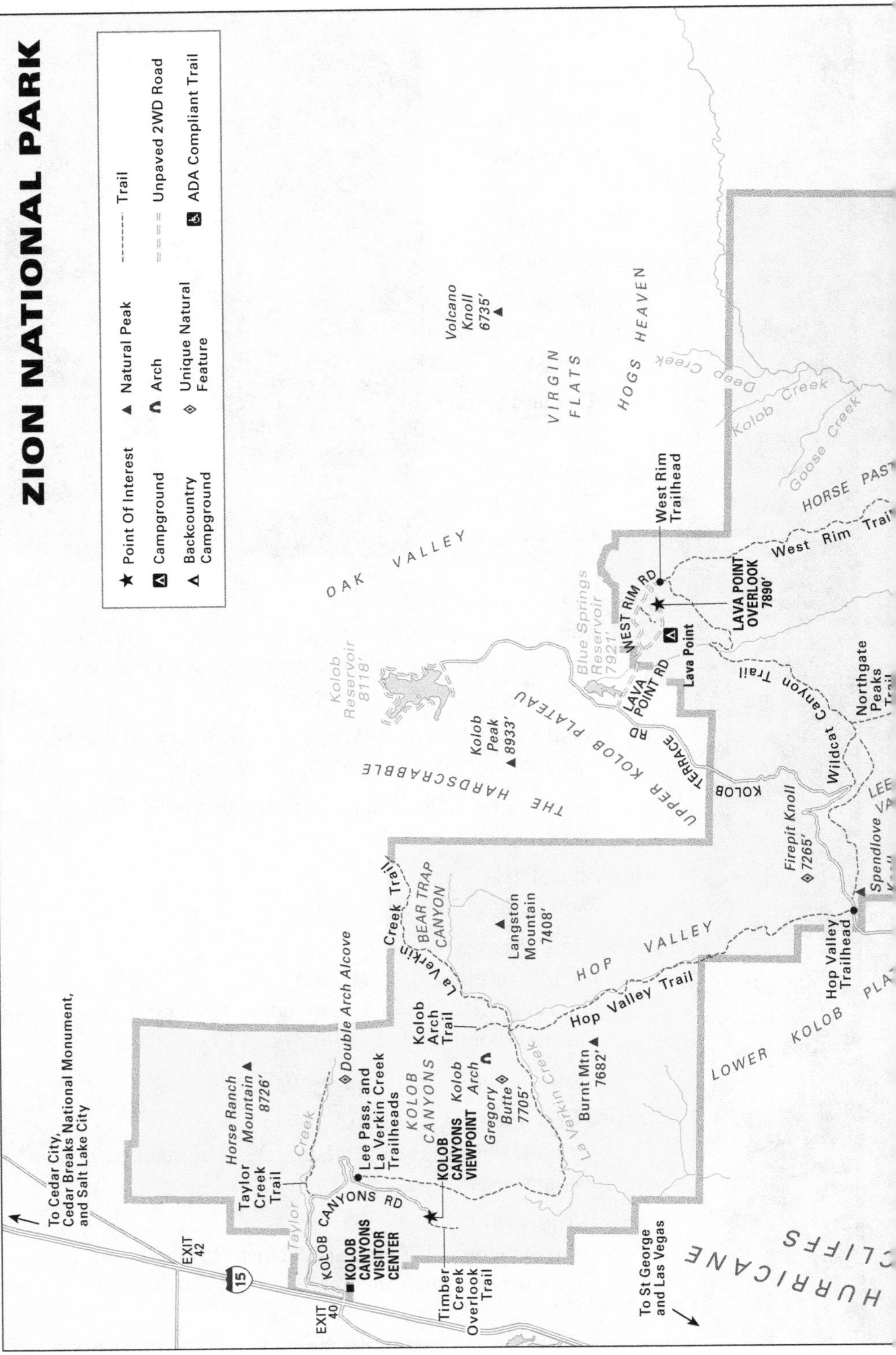

ZION NATIONAL PARK

Legend:
- ★ Point Of Interest
- ▲ Campground
- ▲ Backcountry Campground
- ▲ Natural Peak
- ∩ Arch
- ◈ Unique Natural Feature
- ------- Trail
- = = = Unpaved 2WD Road
- ♿ ADA Compliant Trail

To Cedar City, Cedar Breaks National Monument, and Salt Lake City

EXIT 42

EXIT 40

15

Horse Ranch Mountain ▲ 8726'

Taylor Creek Trail

Taylor Creek

◈ Double Arch Alcove

Creek Trail

La Verkin Creek Trail

BEAR TRAP CANYON

KOLOB CANYONS RD

Lee Pass, and La Verkin Creek Trailheads

KOLOB CANYONS VISITOR CENTER

Timber Creek Overlook Trail

KOLOB CANYONS VIEWPOINT

★ Kolob Arch Trail

KOLOB CANYONS

Kolob Arch ∩

Gregory ◈ Butte 7705'

Langston Mountain 7408'

La Verkin Creek

Burnt Mtn ▲ 7682'

HOP VALLEY

Hop Valley Trail

Firepit Knoll ◈ 7265'

Hop Valley Trailhead

To St George and Las Vegas

HURRICANE CLIFFS

Kolob Reservoir 8118'

Blue Springs Reservoir 7921'

OAK VALLEY

Kolob Peak ▲ 8933'

THE HARDSCRABBLE

UPPER KOLOB PLATEAU

WEST RIM RD

LAVA POINT RD

KOLOB TERRACE RD

▲ Lava Point

LAVA POINT OVERLOOK 7890'

West Rim Trailhead

West Rim Trail

Wildcat Canyon Trail

Northgate Peaks Trail

KOLOB

Spendlove

LEE

LOWER KOLOB PLA

Volcano Knoll 6735' ▲

VIRGIN FLATS

HOGS HEAVEN

Kolob Creek

Goose Creek

Deep Creek

HORSE PAST

96

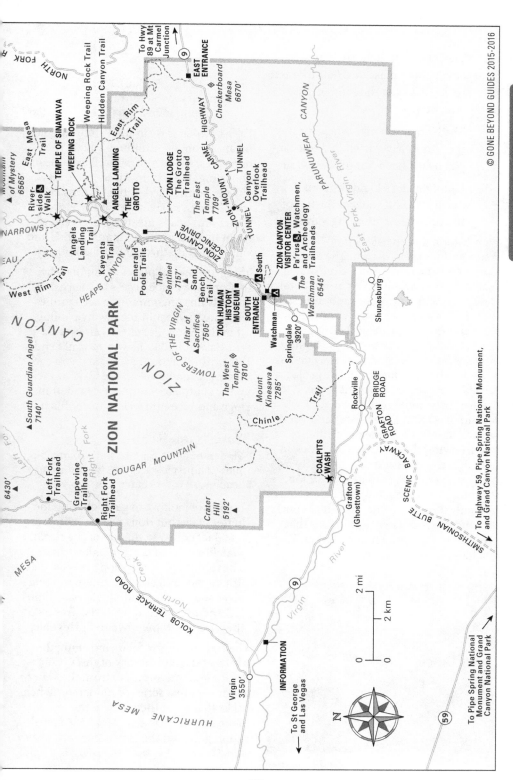

© GONE BEYOND GUIDES 2015-2016

NORTH FORK F

To Hwy 89 at Mt Carmel Junction

EAST ENTRANCE

9

Weeping Rock Trail

Hidden Canyon Trail

TEMPLE OF SINAWAVA

WEEPING ROCK

East Rim Trail

East Mesa Trail

Mountain of Mystery 6565'

Checkerboard Mesa 6670'

ZION LODGE

The Grotto Trailhead

ANGELS LANDING

THE GROTTO

ZION-MOUNT CARMEL HIGHWAY

TUNNEL

TUNNEL

The East Temple 7709'

Canyon Overlook Trailhead

Riverside Walk

Angels Landing Trail

Kayenta Trail

ZION CANYON SCENIC DRIVE

NARROWS

West Rim Trail

Emerald Pools Trails

HEAPS CANYON

The Sentinel 7115'

Sand Bench Trail

ZION CANYON VISITOR CENTER

Pa'rus, Watchmen, and Archeology Trailheads

South

PARUNUWEAP CANYON

East Fork Virgin River

EAU

CANYON

ZION NATIONAL PARK

TOWERS OF THE VIRGIN

Altar of Sacrifice 7505'

ZION HUMAN HISTORY MUSEUM

SOUTH ENTRANCE

The Watchman 6545'

Shunesburg

South Guardian Angel 7140'

ZION

The West Temple 7810'

Mount Kinesava 7285'

Watchman

Springdale 3920'

Trail

Chinle

Left Fork

Right Fork

6430'

Left Fork Trailhead

Grapevine Trailhead

Right Fork Trailhead

COUGAR MOUNTAIN

Crater Hill 5192'

COALPITS WASH

Rockville

BRIDGE ROAD

GRAFTON ROAD

Grafton (Ghosttown)

SMITHSONIAN BUTTE SCENIC BACKWAY

To highway 59, Pipe Spring National Monument, and Grand Canyon National Park

MESA

KOLOB TERRACE ROAD

North Creek

Virgin River

HURRICANE MESA

Virgin 3550'

INFORMATION

To St George and Las Vegas

N

2 mi

2 km

0

0

9

59

To Pipe Spring National Monument and Grand Canyon National Park

What Makes Zion Special

- The afternoon light striking wall after wall of massive 2,000-foot red rock cliffs extending into a deep river canyon

- The Narrows, a hike whose trail is the Virgin River itself in a slot canyon over fifteen hundred feet tall

- Hiking Angels Landing, a hike hewn into cliff walls to the top of the canyon for stunning views

Zion National Park has a lot of "Wow" factor and for good reason. The entire Colorado Plateau was once a massive sand dune in line with the current Sarah Desert. As with any set of sand dunes, there is one area where the winds are just right and the dunes are at their highest. For the Colorado Plateau, those highest dunes were where Zion sits today and as a result, when the mechanics of geology turned those dunes into sandstone, it left the area with some really big chunks of rock to play with. Enter water and wind, which cut into the stone over millions of years, leaving sheer cliffs of epic rock in hues of reds, oranges and tans. There are many singular words to describe Zion, stunning, humbling, majestic, and even heavenly. Whatever one word that comes to mind, there are really no words that give this place a proper description. You just have to go and see it.

Angels Landing

Hiking in the Main Park

Pa'rus Trail

Easy – (3.5 mi / 5.6 km), round trip, allow 2 hours, elev. Δ: 50 ft / 15 m, trailheads at South Campground and Canyon Junction

Pa'rus, which is from the Paiute language, means bubbling, tumbling water. The name describes this trail well as it meanders along the Virgin River. The trail is paved and thus accessible for those with wheelchairs. Pa'rus starts at the visitor center and heads upstream at a very slight incline. The surrounding cliffs and valley open up throughout the journey.

There are several places along the way that provide beach access to the river and it is not uncommon to see families enjoying the heat of the day by cooling off in the water. Pa'rus trail crosses six bridges as it makes its way to trail's end at Canyon Junction. From here you can hike back (downhill all the way) or pick up the shuttle to your next destination. Dogs and bikes are welcome on this trail.

Watchman Trail

Moderate – (3.3 mi / 5.3 km), round trip, allow 2 hours, elev. Δ: 368 ft / 112 m, trailhead near visitor center

If you are looking to get higher up for better views but don't want to climb the 2,000 feet or so to the top of the rim, the Watchman Trail is a good alternative. The trail starts at the Zion Canyon Visitor Center and ends at a mesa top that gives some commanding views of Zion NP and even a glimpse of the Towers of the Virgin and the town of Springdale.

The trail begins by following along the banks of the North Fork of the Virgin River and then juts away from the water to connect to a series of moderate switchbacks that wind their way to the top of the mesa. There is a nominal 368 feet elevation gain, but the views are worth every step. Once at the mesa top there is a half-

Sunrise in Zion Canyon

mile loop that walks around the edge. Note that the loop mileage isn't listed as part of the distance noted in the NPS hiking guide. This is a popular trail due to both the views and the fact it starts at the visitor center.

Archeology Trail

Easy – (0.4 mi / 0.6 km), round trip, allow 0.5 hour, elev. Δ: 80 ft / 24 m, trailhead near visitor center

The Archeology Trail is a great hike if you are looking for an early evening stroll. The trail is short, less than half a mile (0.6 kilometers), but climbs fairly steadily to a 1000-year-old prehistoric storage site. While the site requires a fair amount of imagination to piece together the history, this is not the only reason for going.

The site is close to the Watchman campground and rises to a nice vantage point in a very short distance. One can take in phenomenal views both up and down the canyon. You will notice the green riparian corridor of the Virgin River as it meanders through an ever-widening canyon. In all, this is a short but worthwhile trek you can take if you are looking for something near camp.

Sand Bench Trail

Moderate – (7.6 mi / 12.2 km), round trip, allow 5 hours, elev. Δ: 466 ft / 142 m, trailhead at Zion Lodge or Court of the Patriarchs shuttle stops

This long ambling trail follows along Birch Creek before climbing up to a long and decent sized plateau named Sand Bench. The trail does have a 466-foot elevation gain but for the most part, the gain is felt primarily as you ascend to the plateau.

Start at the Court of the Patriarchs shuttle stop and pick up the Sand Bench Trail as it follows from the Virgin River up Birch Creek. The trail then heads up to and runs the length of the Sand Bench plateau. As the hike unfolds, the Patriarchs, East Temple, Streaked Wall, Sentinel, Mountain of the Sun, and many other peaks can be seen. This trail is shared with horse riders, so be mindful as you take in the views.

Lower Emerald Pool Trail

Easy – (1.2 mi / 1.9 km), round trip, allow 1 hour,, elev. Δ: 69 ft / 21 m, trailhead at Zion Lodge shuttle stop

There are two trails described in the Zion hiking guide that make up the Emerald Pools, the lower pools and upper pools. Lower Emerald Pools is flat, is paved much of the way, is short in distance and provides incredible views of waterfalls and shallow pools. You do climb a bit on the lower trail, which allows for some nice views of the valley.

The two pools on the lower trail are nice enough, but as is almost always the case, the best pool is at the top. As the canyon is surrounded on both sides by steep cliffs, it will be well into morning before the sun hits the western side of the canyon. By mid-afternoon, the sun will have passed over the other side, providing more shade. In warm weather, plan on hitting the trail either in early morning or late afternoon to stay cool.

Upper Emerald Pool Trail

Moderate – (1.0 mi / 1.6 km), round trip from lower pools, allow 1 hour, elev. Δ: 200 ft / 61 m, trailhead at Zion Lodge shuttle stop

Here the trail continues from the Lower Emerald Pool Trail for the final mile. The paved trail is now dirt and the trail climbs more steeply. If you are doing this trail in the morning, the sun may have passed over the monolith walls and is now part of the climb up. The views do get better as you gain elevation, and the pool at the top is by far the biggest, sitting at the base of the western cliff faces. It is well worth the effort for the views. These pools are not intended for swimming.

Kayenta Trail

Moderate – (2.0 mi / 3.2 km), round trip, allow 2 hours, elev. Δ: 150 ft / 46 m, trailhead at Grotto shuttle stop

Kayenta Trail is often done along with the Grotto Trail and the Emerald Pools Trail to create a loop. The trail is great

in its own right, giving some great views deeper into the canyon near the Zion Lodge. The trail has a small 150-foot elevation gain.

Waterfall at Emerald Pools

The trail can be picked up easily from The Grotto shuttle stop. From the shuttle stop cross the Virgin River via a bridge and follow along its upper banks for a short distance. The trail then enters into Behunin Canyon from the North side before meeting up with the Emerald Pools Trail. To make a loop of it, continue along and down the Emerald Pools Trail until it ends at the Zion Lodge and then pick up the Grotto Trail back to where you started.

The Grotto Trail

Easy – (1.0 mi / 1.6 km), round trip, allow 30 minutes, elev. Δ: 35 ft / 11 m, trailhead at Grotto shuttle stop

The Grotto Trail is a simple little flat jaunt that connects the Zion Lodge with the Grotto Picnic Area. It is used by many to connect the Emerald and Kayenta Trails to make a 2 ½ mile loop. The Grotto area itself contains picnic tables and grates for grilling. It also contains the Grotto Museum, which is the oldest building in Zion. If you are a fan of the historical stonework of the Zion Lodge, be sure to include the Grotto Trail to the mix to see both the museum and the artist in residence house.

Angels Landing via West Rim Trail

Strenuous – (5.4 mi / 8.7 km), round trip, allow 4-5 hours, elev. Δ: 1,488 ft / 453 m, trailhead at Grotto shuttle stop

The views are unparalleled from the unique Angels Landing trail. Built during the wake of the Great Depression by the CCC, it comprises a series of switchbacks cut into solid rock. The final half mile is along a narrow knife-edged ridge that uses chains and carved footholds to assist you to the final destination. It is strenuous, but the end result is well worth it. You will have climbed from the bottom of the canyon to close to the top, giving you a view that will most certainly become a life moment. It is a world famous hike and one of the most popular in Zion.

The trail's name was coined by Frederick Fisher in 1916 when he looked up at the monolith and exclaimed, "only and angel could land on it." With the help of the CCC, (Frederick Fisher) forged a trail to the top.

The trail is composed of six distinct parts. The first follows a paved path along the river before dog legging west from the river toward a cliff wall. If you look carefully at this point in the trail, you will see the second portion of the journey, a series of switchbacks up this cliff wall. Even from a distance, the switchbacks are impressive if not audacious. The trail builders carved a fairly wide paved trail into solid rock and while you are indeed climbing up a cliff face, this portion is merely strenuous and no more dangerous than any well-established trail with exposure.

There is a reprieve at the third portion. At the top of the switchbacks, the trail goes between two massive monolithic columns through what is aptly named Refrigerator Canyon. The monoliths climb high enough to block out the sun and there is a cool breeze that greets visitors as soon as they reach the top of the switchbacks. This lasts for only a short half mile before you arrive at the fourth portion, called Walter's Wiggles. The Wiggles are a series of 21 short but consistently steep switchbacks that wind back and forth until you get to the next respite, called Scout's Lookout.

The lookout is the fifth portion of the journey and a great place to take a rest. The Wiggles are below you and from the lookout, you can see the final half mile pitch ahead of you to Angels Landing. The area offers incredible views. There is also a pit toilet and plenty of places to relax before your final leg. Up to this point you have been on the West Rim Trail, so make sure you follow the signs to the top of Angels Landing, as the West Rim Trail does continue onward.

The final pitch is a bit exciting as it has the adventure of chains that you can grab onto to ensure you get up the last leg. This portion is a razor back ridge. It is fairly narrow with steep drop offs on either side. The trail is well marked by the chains and crosses the back of the ridge several times as you climb. Many hikers have made this journey and in the end, it is not as scary as it sounds. That said, this is not a place to test yourself; a handful of people have fallen to their deaths on this trail. I've seen teenagers on this trail but only two children who were in the single digit age bracket. Use caution, for both yourself and your fellow hikers.

Once at the top, there is a somewhat narrow but flat area to take in the lofty vista. To the north is a grand view of the end of Zion Canyon. You will find yourself gazing at an enormous cul-de-sac of towering rock. As the eye travels from the edge of Angels Landing down the canyon, the citadel of rock stands as one complete sentry extending to the horizon. The red cliff walls meet the green of the desert, culminating in a dense riparian snake of vegetation that surrounds the Virgin River. At times swallows soaring at incredible speeds up to 40 miles per hour (64 km/hour) can be seen. They will soar seemingly straight into the cliff walls only to stop at the last second and land in their nests.

Weeping Rock Trail

Easy – (0.4 mi / 0.6 km), round trip, allow 30 minutes, elev. Δ: 98 ft / 30 m, trailhead at Weeping Rock shuttle stop

This is a short paved trail that ends at an alcove called Weeping Rock. True to its name, water seeps through the sandstone and then falls gently like a soft rain once it reaches the overhang. It is possible to stand underneath and watch the magic of water and stone, even on a sunny day. The trail is great for kids and casual hikers looking for a great view of the Great White Throne. There is about 100 feet of elevation gain and some trailside exhibits.

Hidden Canyon Trail

Strenuous – (2.4 mi / 3.9 km), round trip, allow 2-3 hours, elev. Δ: 850 ft / 259 m, trailhead at Weeping Rock shuttle stop

If you don't mind exposure to steep drop offs, this is a really cool hike. Mind you, there are long drops and chains are put in places to assist in some areas, so if you do have a fear of heights, this trail may not be for you. Hidden Canyon starts from the Weeping Rock shuttle and follows a paved trail steeply upwards along a set of well-constructed switchbacks. At the trail junction for Hidden Canyon, East Rim Trail and Observation Point, keep to the right and head up a series of short and steep switchbacks not unlike Walters Wiggles found over at Angels Landing.

Climbing up Angels Landing

After the switchbacks, the trail clings at various times to the edge of a steeply sloping rock face. In some areas there are chains to assist the hiker, in others, the trail looks a little intimidating but is wide and safe enough. In one part, steps have been carved directly into the sandstone. This whole part of the hike is akin to being Indiana Jones looking for some ancient treasure. This is truly a fun and exhilarating hike. That said, if you aren't a fan of heights, this might not be the best trail.

The hike ends at the mouth of Hidden Canyon. With some basic scrambling, it is possible to continue up the canyon a bit to a small 10-foot arch along a sandy stream-bed section of the trip. Hidden Canyon throws off a lot of the visitors due to its exposure and while it can be dangerous under wet conditions, is quite fine for those who have figured out how far to trust the grip of sandstone un-der one's feet. The other

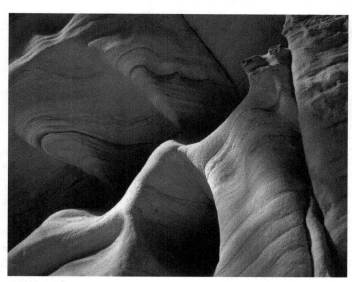

The magic of color at Zion

plus is the hike is typically in the shade for most of the day, which helps in the heat of the summer. Elevation gain for this trail is 800 feet.

East Rim Trail

Strenuous – (10.6 mi / 17.1 km), one way, allow 6 – 7 hours, elev. Δ: 1,365 ft / 415 m, two trailheads, described below

Like the West Rim Trail, most hikers start at the upper end with the descent in front of them. For this trail, that is done by starting at the East Rim Trailhead, located at the Zion East Entrance Ranger Station and heading to the Weeping Rock shuttle stop. This is a great backpacking

destination due to the numerous spur trails, including Deertrap Mountain and Cable Mountain Trails.

Starting from the East Entrance, views of Checkboard Mesa and the head of Jolly Gulch can be seen. This initial portion of the trail does have some elevation gain as the trail navigates the contour of the pla-teau. There are some very dramatic views along this portion. At 6 miles in there is a trail to the left that leads to Cable Mountain and Deertrap Trails as well as a trail junction farther on for Observation Point. The trail then comes to the top of Echo Canyon, where it heads swiftly downwards 1,000 feet (see Observation Point for more details here).

Observation Point via East Rim Trail

Strenuous – (8.0 mi / 12.9 km), round trip, allow 6 hours, elev. Δ: 2,148 ft / 655 m, trailhead at Weeping Rock shuttle stop

Okay, if you found yourself wanting to get to the top of Zion Canyon from the moment you arrived, this is one of the trails that will get you there. The trail climbs some 2,148 feet over four miles with some serious drop offs along the way and is all done in full sun. While strenuous, this is a hike to remember.

Start at the Weeping Rock shuttle stop and proceed up the shared trail to Hidden Canyon, East Rim Trail, and Observation Point following a series of well-built switchbacks. At the junction, stay left and continue through Echo Canyon, a narrow and steep canyon with little pools of running water carved into the sandstone. As the climb continues, the trail starts to bring the white Temple Cap formation closer into view. Zion Canyon, Angels Landing, Cathedral Mountain, and Three Patriarchs are in full view. The views from the top as well as the trip through Echo Canyon make this steep hike well worth the effort.

Cable Mountain Trail

Strenuous – (17.5 mi / 28.2 km from East Entrance), round trip, allow 8-10 hours, elev. Δ: up 1,000 ft, down 2,000 ft

Strenuous (15.5 mi / 25.0 km from Weeping Rock shuttle stop), round trip, allow 7-9 hours, elev. Δ: 2,100 ft / 640 m

Moderate (7.5 mi / 12.1 km from Zion Ponderosa Ranch, round trip, allow 5 hours, elev. Δ: 300 ft / 91 m

There are three ways to get to Cable Mountain Trail. See the trail descriptions for Observation Point and East Rim Trail for additional information on the routes to Cable Mountain Trail. For the Zion Ponderosa Ranch route, head out to the East Entrance and make a left to North Fork Road. Follow the signs to Zion Ponderosa and once at the resort, look for signs to Cable Mountain Trail, making a left at the main entrance, and then going straight past the resort buildings. The trailhead connects with the East Rim Trail and onwards to Cable Mountain Trail.

In 1901, there was a tram that carried lumber from the top of Zion Canyon to the valley floor. This engineering marvel, built by pioneer David Flanigan contained 3,300 feet of cable and could supply lumber to the valley floor in several minutes, which was a massive improvement over the 3-day journey by wagon that it took prior. Many of the original buildings in Zion were built with this lumber. The frameworks were destroyed twice by fire and in 1930; the park service removed the cables. The draw works still sits at the top of Cable Mountain at the end of the trail.

Deertrap Trail

Strenuous – (19.5 mi / 31.4 km from East Entrance), round trip, allow 11-12 hours,, elev. Δ: up 1,000 ft, down 2,000 ft

Strenuous (17.5 mi / 28.2 km from Weeping Rock shuttle stop), round trip, allow 8-10 hours, elev. Δ: 2,100 ft / 640 m

Moderate (9.5 mi / 15.3 km from Zion Ponderosa Ranch, round trip, allow 6 hours, elev. Δ: 300 ft / 91 m

This is certainly a long day hike or as an add on within the East Rim Trail. Use the East Rim, Observation Point and Cable Mountain Trail descriptions to initiate the three routes, as appropriate.

Once on the side trail from East Rim Trail, continue past Cable Mountain Trail for another two miles to a series of overlooks collectively referred to as a sky island. Each view is slightly different, offering expansive views into the north and south portions of Zion Canyon as well as the outer peaks and terrain.

Canyon Overlook Trail

Moderate – (1.0 mi / 1.6 km), round trip, allow 1 hour, elev. Δ: 163 ft / 50 m, trailhead near east Zion Tunnel entrance

This is another in the list of "great views without too much effort" category. The trail starts right before the Zion Tunnel as you head into the park. There are parking lots on either side of the Zion-Mount Carmel Highway. The trail gets a fair amount of "impulse hiking" as folks wait for the directed traffic of the tunnel to open up. After all, hiking in Zion does beat out being stuck in traffic in Zion. The hike has a modest 163-foot elevation gain and climbs some steps cut into the sandstone. At the end of the trail is an overlook with a railing at the cliff's edge giving great views of the lower portions of Zion Canyon and Pine Creek immediately below, as well as an interesting perspective of the Zion Tunnel.

Riverside Walk

Easy – (2.2 mi / 3.5 km), round trip, allow 90 minutes, elev. Δ: 57 ft / 17 m, trailhead at Temple of Sinawava shuttle stop

Riverside Walk starts at roads end of the wide main portion of the Zion box canyon. From here, the canyon begins to narrow but is still wide enough for the paved Riverside Walk trail that meanders until it reaches The Narrows proper. The trail is fairly flat, with several rolling ups and downs as it contours to the land. There are also a few spots with watery grottoes as well as multiple spots for river beach access. The trail ends at a stonework terrace where you can gaze at the mouth of The Narrows and the various hikers beginning or ending their hike of this landmark trek.

The Narrows

Imagine walking up a river flowing clearly and gently around your feet. At times there is no shore, only river and massive sandstone walls that run from the edge of the water and rise swiftly straight up 2000 feet into the sky. There are places where the canyon is wide enough to permit a view of distant sandstone monoliths and other places where the canyon is delightfully slender, only 20-30 feet wide. Each turn gives a different view, all wondrous and grand. For a bit, the river stretches out, allowing a chance to walk on soft sand. You see deer grazing on the banks. Waterfalls come sliding down

curved walls from unreachable heights. There is no trail but the river. If you think about it, each step up and down is a step no one has ever taken before in exactly the same way.

Be warned, it is possible that you won't be able to hike the Narrows. If the Virgin River is running too high, either due to winter/spring runoff or to summer flash floods, you will not be able to go on this hike. That said, if the river is running favorably, then make it a point to add this to your itinerary. The park service actively controls access to the Narrows, which does take the guesswork out of the safety of hiking this trail.

Going Upstream from the Bottom of the Canyon

Easy to Strenuous – (9.4 mi / 15.1 km), round trip, allow up to 8 hours depending on distance traveled, elev. Δ: 334 ft / 102 m, trailhead at Temple of Sinawava shuttle stop

Into the Narrows

SOUTHWEST UTAH

Zion

The Narrows is found by taking the shuttle to the very end of the canyon via the Riverside Walk Trail. It will take about 40–45 minutes from the campground to the end of the canyon via the shuttle. It will take another hour to 90 minutes to walk the 2.2 miles (3.5 km) needed to complete the Riverside Walk Trail. Make sure you add in this time when you plan your hike.

The Riverside Walk Trail is flat, easy and paved. The trail follows the Virgin River up along its banks, and there are plenty of places to drop off the trail to explore the river itself. At the end of the trail is a small set of steps down to the river where The Narrows begins and where the hike gets really interesting.

There are a few trails, but for the most part, you walk in the river itself. You will be walking upstream on uneven ground at times, so be prepared to get wet. Depending on how far up you decide to go, you will need to wade and even swim in some stretches. If you feel confident that the trail will be open, it's best to pick up

water shoes beforehand and bring them on the trip for this hike. It will make your hike more enjoyable.

Depending on the time of year, the water may be swift and cold. In the summer, usually by June, the river slows down to a steady but not terribly swift pace, and the temperature is more refreshing than cold.

There are restrictions to how far up you are allowed to travel upstream without a permit. There is a tributary creek called Orderville Junction, which is a common destination for most hikers and is the limit of how far up you can travel without a permit. Orderville Junction is about two hours from the trail. That said, it is possible to never make it this far and still have an amazing hike. Each bend offers a different experience and new view with another bend at the end that beckons you farther.

Returning will take slightly less time since you are going downstream with the flow of water. If you are doing the hike in late afternoon, make a note of when

If You Hike the Narrows

- Have a full understanding of the weather before you go. Flash floods can originate from storms that aren't close to where you are hiking.

- Carry a gallon of water per person and some food, sunscreen and a first aid kit.

- Bring a pullover if the weather is temperate. It is colder in the canyon.

- Bring waterproof bags for cameras and other items that you need to keep dry.

- The only restroom on the hike is at the beginning of the Riverside Walk. There are no other places

to go, even if you "have to." This is a popular destination and there are no discreet bushes. Make sure everyone goes prior to beginning the hike.

- Walking sticks are preferred by most folks for added stability, as are sturdy hiking boots. Water shoes and tennis shoes are okay for the casual hike up river. Sandals are not recommended though hiking sandals are okay.

- This is not a great hike for young children. My 9-year-old did fine, but keep in mind it is over two miles of walking just to get to the beginning of The Narrows. While the current is typically fine for adults, it may be too much for smaller ones.

you start the hike from the shuttle drop off and how much time you have left before sunset. If you have 3 hours, hike up for 90 minutes and turn around. The Narrows is not an easy hike in the dark especially if you don't have a flashlight.

Going Downstream from the Top of the Canyon

Strenuous – (16 mi / 25.7 km), one way, full day hike, elev. Δ: 1,400 ft / 427 m, trailhead at Zion Narrows parking area

Going downstream can be done with a National Park Service wilderness permit. Allow a full day for this 16-mile hike. You can find private jeep shuttles that regularly go up to the drop off spot. This is a strenuous day's hike. There are ample stories of folks that find themselves having to stick it out for the night because they thought it would be an easier hike. Hiking in streambeds is slow work and is more tiring than walking on even pavement. Underestimating this hike in the wrong conditions can be dangerous as well. Flash floods and exposure from the night's elements are serious matters.

West Temple and Altar of Sacrifice

Chinle Trail

Strenuous – (6.8 mi / 10.9 km), round trip to Huber Wash, allow 3 – 5 hours, elev. Δ: 650 ft / 198 m, two trailheads off SR-9

This is a very different hike than most of Zion, showing off the diversity of Lowland Desert Ecology as well as crossing through a petrified forest. The trail is well exposed and will be very hot in the full sun of summer. The trail is more wel-

coming in spring and fall, with wildflowers present in the spring.

The hike has two trailhead entrances, both from Highway 9. The entrance closest to the town of Springdale requires parking in the designated lot labeled "Trailhead Parking". Parking in the subdivision will get you towed. From the trailhead wind through the local neighborhood to the park's boundary and continue through a forested area with absolutely remarkable views. After 3.2 miles, the trail meets up with Huber Wash. Head back from here.

It is also possible to continue to make this somewhat of a loop trail; however, as some of the loop is Highway 9, it's best to have two cars. Taking the full loop to Coalpits Wash from Chinle Trailhead is a total of 15 miles.

Right Fork Trailhead

Strenuous – (10.6 mi / 17.1 km), round trip from bottom up, allow 8 – 12 hours, elev. Δ: 1,000 ft / 300 m, trailhead on Kolob Terrace Road

Like the Left Fork Trailhead, this is more route than maintained trail. The first couple of miles were hit by a fire in 2006 and the area is in a cycle of recovery. The hike within the streambed is pretty slow going, so allow extra time. That said, while the Right Fork is a bit more rugged to navigate, the scenery is quite peaceful and meandering with the route ending at a set of pretty incredible double waterfalls. Like the Left Fork, this trail can get hot in the summer despite the lure of water.

Start the hike at the Right Fork Trailhead on Kolob Terrace Road. The first quarter mile crosses the fire area to a bluff overlooking North Creek. From here head steeply down and into the creek bed. Do make note of this entrance, as it is easy to miss on the way out. Once at North Creek, start heading upstream passing the confluence of Left Fork. Cross the stream on the left side here and follow the path that crisscrosses the creek multiple times.

At about 2.5 miles into the hike, pass Trail Canyon on the right. A short spur trip up this canyon about one quarter of a mile will lead to a set of cascades. Back in North Creek, at close to 4 miles in, the hiker will encounter a very cool five-foot waterfall pouring through the slickrock into a nice pool. About a half mile further up, the canyon narrows and holds multiple waterfalls, pools, and hanging gardens. Further up another mile is Double Falls, another picturesque set of cascades.

From here, the end of the journey without ropes is Barrier Falls, about a third of a mile further upstream. The going here is tougher, requiring one to scramble up slick rock, bushwhack and otherwise navigate slowly to the falls. There is a set of falls in between, but you will know you are at Barrier Falls, its name holds true.

Unlike the Left Fork Trail, a permit is not required for Right Fork. Coming back, be glad you made note of the trail you came down as getting back up to the rim without the trail can be dangerous.

Left Fork Trailhead

Strenuous – (7.0 mi / 11.3 km), round trip, allow 5 - 8 hours, elev. Δ: 1,000 ft / 300 m, trailhead on Kolob Terrace Road

The Left Fork of North Creek is most popular for a stretch labeled The Subway, a short and rather amazing section of the creek that looks more like a worm tunnel than a streambed. This is one of the best hikes in the park and is more route than actual trail. The whole journey is alongside and often in the creek, which makes for slow going. Unlike The Narrows, which can be cooler in the summer heat, this hike is definitely a hot hike when temperatures are high. Start early if it looks to be a hot day.

The Subway

It is possible to enter from the top and make your way down stream, but this is longer and requires a bit of rappelling and swimming (and carrying your rappelling gear). A permit is required no matter which direction you travel. From bottom to top is described here.

From the bottom, the trail starts by picking ones way down a 400 foot gully starting from the Left Fork Trailhead on Kolob Terrace Road. Once in the creek, head upstream for about two to three hours. The Subway section is a tight section of the creek with several twists and turns right above a cascading set of falls called Red Waterfalls. The Subway itself is spectacular with clear pools and an almost subterranean feel.

It is possible to continue upwards but be mindful of time. Shortly after The Subway you will be met with large black pools that you must swim to get across to continue exploring the slot canyon. Further up is a soothing little waterfall with a secret natural room behind a watery curtain. Journeying from here requires bouldering and rappelling experience. Enjoy and head back down before dark.

Like The Narrows, this slot canyon does experience extreme changes in water volume due to flash floods. The permit process helps provide education along the way for this route, but do enter well informed as to the weather for the day.

The unbelievable view from top of Angels Landing

Hiking in the Kolob Canyon Section

Hop Valley Trail

Strenuous – (15 mi / 24.1 km), round trip, allow 10 hours, elev. Δ: 1,050 ft / 320 m, trailhead off Kolob Terrace Road

The Hop Valley Trail, located in the Kolob Canyons section of Zion is typically done as part of the Trans Zion hike, a 48 mile, 5-day trek that crosses Zion from the Kolobs at Lee Pass to the East Rim. Lacking the fame of the main Zion and Kolob Canyons, the Hop Valley trail is a hidden gem. It is possible to use Hop Valley as a longer and more remote method to Kolob Arch. The route described here is from Kolob Terrace Road to Kolob Arch and back.

From the Hop Valley Trailhead on Kolob Terrace Road pick up the northern trailhead into Hop Valley. The trail starts out in a wide and open valley filled with deep sand and plenty of sagebrush. Walking in deep sand is a consistent trait of this trail. In areas, grazing has left its mark on the vegetation. As you continue, the valley narrows and travel is along a pleasant stream. The trail does have a fair amount of creek crossings; look for NPS trail markers to keep you on the trail. Campsites are about five miles in at an NPS boundary gate. The vegetation is more pristine once you cross into

the park. Take a series of switchbacks downhill to connect to La Verkin Creek and follow it downstream to the Kolob Arch Viewpoint.

Overall, this hike has about 1,000 feet elevation gain, mostly felt on the return. That said, the trail is more strenuous due to its length than the elevation.

Northgate Peaks Trail

Easy – (4.5 mi / 7.2 km), round trip, allow 3 hours, elev. Δ: 50 ft / 15 m, trailhead off Wildcat Canyon trail

If you wondered if you could find a hike that wasn't too hard but also wasn't shared with millions of other tourists, this trail is a good bet. Northgate Peaks Trail is off the beaten path and isn't in the popular NPS hiking brochures so it doesn't get as much traffic. The hike also shows a different view of Zion, ambling through large ponderosa pine forests found in the higher elevations. The hike is cooler and walks amongst the white Temple Cap monoliths dotting the landscape.

While the name of this there and back hike makes it sound like it climbs some massive Zion mountain, the elevation gain is only 250 feet. The trail ends at a craggy volcanic knob offering views that

Kolob Canyon

are distinctively different from the main portions of Zion and the Kolob Canyons. Access to Northgate Peaks Trail is from the Wildcat Canyon parking lot on Kolob Terrace Road.

Wildcat Canyon Trail

Moderate – (12.0 mi / 19.3 km), round trip, allow 4-7 hours, elev. Δ: 450 ft / 137 m, two trailheads off Kolob Terrace Road

Normally done as a connector trail, this is a great day hike in its own right. The hike is incredibly pleasant with only modest elevation gain/loss. The trail passes through groves of ponderosa pines and high meadows before dropping down into Wildcat Canyon. The trail offers a leisurely way to see the country-side, with plenty of opportunities to find wildflowers and wildlife along the way. This trail is not the standard Zion high red rock cliffs and there are no striking viewpoints to be found at trail's end, but the entire feel that the journey is the destination is what makes this hike so special.

West Rim Trailhead

Strenuous – (12.9 – 14.4 mi / 20.7 – 23.1 km), one way, allow 10 hours, elev. Δ: 3,600 ft / 1097 m, trailhead at Lava Point

This is a long day hike or a pleasant overnight backpacking trip. The hike is best if started from the West Rim

Trailhead at Kolob Terrace Road and heading towards the other end at The Grotto shuttle stop. Since the shuttle doesn't go to both ends of the trail, you will need a means of transportation back to your car.

Starting near Lava Point on Kolob Terrace Road pick up the trail and keep straight to avoid the Wildcat Canyon Trail. The trail heads along the Horse Plateau through sparsely forested ponderosa pines. After 4.5 miles, the trail descends into a happy little meadow named Potato Hollow. Here there is a small pond and a spring that is usually running. This is a good place to relax and fill up canteens, (be sure to treat or filter). There are some great views into Imlay canyon by taking a short side spur to the east.

The trail then climbs about 500 feet out of the hollow and back onto Horse Plateau proper over a distance of 1.5 miles. At this point, the hike offers two routes. There is the primary West Rim Trail, which is 1.5 miles longer, and the Telephone Canyon Trail. The West Rim variation gives great views of Phantom Valley and the southern Zion canyons. The Telephone Canyon variation is named by settlers trying to establish a telephone line into Zion Canyon. The route here is shorter and sticks more to the interior of Horse Plateau.

111

Both variations meet up at Cabin Springs, a small seep that collects into a small pool. There are campsites nearby. This water is fine to drink given you filter or treat it and have a strong amount of patience. From Cabin Springs, the real fun begins as the trail heads steeply down into Zion Canyon. There are long drop-offs here, but this is a well-maintained trail. Take the path cut into the slick rock and head downwards until you reach a respite at Lookout Point. From here, the trail is an inverse of what is described for the Angels Landing Trail. Follow down Walters Wiggles, through Refrigerator Canyon and down until you end at The Grotto shuttle stop. It is completely possible and recommended to add the Angels Landing to the journey. If you do, be sure to allow another 45 minutes to the overall duration of the hike.

La Verkin Creek Trail (and Kolob Arch)

Strenuous – (14.0 mi / 22.5 km), round trip, allow 8 hours, elev. Δ: 1,037 ft / 316 m, trailhead at Kolob Canyon Road

La Verkin Creek Trail, in the Kolob Canyons section, is a fun trail all around, offering great views including Kolob Arch, one of the largest free-standing arches on earth. The hike itself does have some elevation gain, a little over 1,000 feet; however, the surroundings are amazing enough to help keep

Kolob Arch

your mind off the inclines. Most folks get a permit and camp overnight; however, it is possible to do this as a long day hike to Kolob Arch.

The trail starts at Lee Pass and crosses in front of the southern portion of the Kolob Canyon cliffs. The trail meets up quickly with Timber Creek and follows along its banks, giving some spectacular views in a pinyon juniper forest setting. After about two miles, the trail veers away from the creek into the woods as it heads towards La Verkin Creek. The trail then descends down into the creek's clear waters, with each step putting you into a more immersive Kolob Canyon experience. Cliffs are now towering around you on either side with the sound of water adding to the magic of this hike.

The end of the trail is Kolob Arch viewpoint where the arch can be seen by hiking up about 150 feet to a viewing area. While the official end of the trail listed here is 7 miles, La Verkin Creek Trail does continue up stream for another two miles. There are many side canyons to explore, some of which require canyoneering techniques that lead to triple waterfalls and other delights. If backpacking, it is possible to connect to the Hop Valley Trail, which leads southeast to the Lower Kolob Plateau.

Timber Creek Overlook Trail

Moderate – (1.0 mi / 1.6 km), round trip, allow 30 minutes, elev. Δ: 100 ft / 30 m, trailhead at end of Kolob Canyon Road

This is one of those trails that could labeled as "Easy" without much argument; however, the park lists it as moderate. It does have a 100-foot elevation gain, but is otherwise a straightforward trail. The trail is picked up at the very end of Kolob Canyon Road. From there the trail follows a small ridgeline to an overlook of Kolob Canyon, looking south. On a clear day, it is possible to see all the way to the north rim of the Grand Canyon.

This trail is located within the Kolob Canyon section. Groups are limited to a maximum size of 12 people at a time. Look for wildflowers in season, which can be abundant on this trail.

Taylor Creek Trail

Moderate – (5.0 mi / 8.0 km), round trip, allow 4 hours, elev. Δ: 470 ft / 143 m, trailhead at Kolob Canyon Road

This trail lies within the Kolob Canyons Wilderness and ambles up the Middle Fork of Taylor Creek. This entire area gets less visitation than the main Zion Canyon and this trail in particular has strict limits on prohibiting groups larger than 12 people. Taylor Creek Trail heads into a narrow box canyon of red Navajo Sandstone along a normally gently flowing creek. There is a welcome interplay of the green vegetation and the red hue of the rocks here and the hike overall is one of delight and wonder. Before the trail begins to fade as it nears the end of the box canyon, look for Double Arch Alcove, an impressive set of alcoves, one on top of the other.

Trans- Zion Hike

Strenuous – (47.3 mi / 76.1 km), one way, allow 3 - 5 days

This hike is a wondrous way to get an immersive multi-day experience that covers the broad spectrum that makes up Zion. The route typically starts from Lee Pass in the Kolobs and cuts down into La Verkin Creek before climbing up to the top of Zion Canyon via the West Rim Trail. From here, the trail heads steeply down, crosses the Zion Valley floor, and heads up the other side via the East Rim.

The trip can be done at a nice pace over five days, but one can hoof it in less. That said, the National Park Service allows camping only in designated areas, so plan your camping junctures carefully. The typical route and stops are given below.

The best part of this trek is there is a net elevation gain of just 325 feet! Don't let that fool you though, one ascends and descends over a whopping 6,000 feet getting to that net elevation number.

Trans-Zion Hike Route:

- La Verkin Trail via Lee Pass Trailhead
- La Verkin Trail to Hop Valley Trail
- Hop Valley Trail to Connector Trail
- Connector Trail to Wildcat Canyon Trail
- Wildcat Canyon Trail to West Rim Trail
- Short side trip to Angels Landing (a must for any Trans Zion hike)
- West Rim Trail down to The Grotto shuttle stop
- Hard core walk or shuttle bus ride to Weeping Rock shuttle stop
- East Rim Trail to East Entrance

Typical Itinerary:

Mileage is approximate, as it will depend on what campsites you get or where designated camping isn't a requirement such as on the East Rim and Echo Canyon, where you can find a campsite.

- Day 1 – 6.9 miles: Camp near Kolob Arch along La Verkin Creek Trail
- Day 2 – 16 miles: Camp at Lava Point Campgrounds or Sawmill Spring
- Day 3 - 8 miles: Camp at West Rim, (Potato Hollow or campsite #6)
- Day 4 – 10 miles: West Rim to Echo Canyon
- Day 5 – 6.5 miles: Exit to East Entrance

Quail Creek State Park

Parks Near Zion

Quail Creek and Sand Hollow State Parks offer camping, relaxation and water filled recreation for those traveling to and from Zion National Park. Both parks are located between St. George, UT and Zion NP on State Route 9. Quail Creek is a bit more on the mellow laid back side, whereas Sand Hollow is all about water filled fun in the middle of the desert.

Official Park Website: http://stateparks.utah.gov/parks/quail-creek//

Visitor Center: (435) 879-2378

Park Accessibility:
- Okay for 2WD and RVs
- Day and Overnight Use

Camping in Park:
- Quail Creek Campground: 22 T/RV, drinking water, restrooms, showers, no hookup, reservable at www.reserveamerica.com/

Lodging and Dining in Park:
- None

Nearest Town with Amenities:
- Washington, UT is 8 mi / 13 km from park

Getting There:
- From St George, UT: Take I-15 North to State Hwy 9 East. Total distance is 17 mi / 27 km to park

What Makes Quail Creek State Park Special

Quail Creek State Park manages a deep reservoir for camping, boating, fishing, and swimming. The park is off Interstate 15 just north of the Highway 9 junction to Zion. Peaceful sweeping views of red rocks with the Pine Valley Mountains in the distance. A good place to stop for the night if you are heading to Zion NP.

Quail Creek Reservoir

Sand Hollow State Park

Official Park Website: http://state-parks.utah.gov/parks/sand-hollow//

Visitor Center:

(435) 680-0715

Park Accessibility:
- Okay for 2WD and RVs
- Day and Overnight Use

Camping in Park:
2 campgrounds in park, all sites reservable at http://utahstateparks.reserveamerica.com

- Westside Campground: 40 + 3 ADA T/RV, drinking water, showers, restrooms, hookups, some pull thru sites, dump station
- Sand Pit Campground: 29 T/RV, drinking water, showers, restrooms, hookups, some pull thru sites, dump station

Lodging and Dining in Park:
- None

Nearest Town with Amenities:
- Washington, UT is 10 mi / 16 km from park

Getting There:
- From St George, UT: Take I-15 North to State Hwy 9 East to Sand Hollow Road. Total distance is 18 mi / 29 km to park

What Makes Sand Hollow State Park Special

Although Sand Hollow is very close to Quail Creek State Park and despite both being water themed recreational parks, Sand Hollow is very different. Whereas Quail Creek is peaceful and serene, with wandering vistas, Sand Hollow is playful and fun amidst red rock formations. There are sand dunes to dig your ATV into as well as slick rock to jump off into the waters below. Besides boating, fishing, and swimming, there are two campgrounds.

Sand Hollow is working through an issue with Swimmer's Itch, an allergic reaction to an otherwise harmless parasite found mainly in the summer months. The problem is more prevalent in the warmer shallower areas and can lead to secondary infections. The issue is unfortunately most prevalent with small children who prefer the shallow ends of the waters. For all the details on Swimmer's Itch, go here for more information: http://stateparks.utah.gov/parks/sand-hollow/swimmers-itch/.

Coral Pink Sand Dunes State Park

Quick Facts

Official Park Website:

http://state-parks.utah.gov/parks/coral-pink/

Visitor Center:

(435) 648-2800

Mid Afternoon at Coral Pink Sand Dunes

Park Accessibility:
- Okay for 2WD and RVs
- ATVs, 4WD needed for some areas
- Day and Overnight Use

Experience Level:
- Family Friendly to Experienced Hiker

Camping in Park:
- Coral Pink Sand Dunes Campground: 16 T/RV plus 1 group site, drinking water, showers, restrooms, no hookups, many pull thru sites, reservable at www.reserveamerica.com/

Lodging and Dining in Park:
- None

Nearest Town with Amenities:
- Kanab, UT is 20 mi / 32 km from park

Getting There:
- From St George, UT: Take I-15 North to State Hwy 9 East/State St to UT-59 South to AZ-389 East to Co Hwy 237 to Co Rd 43. Note that final 4 miles is a dirt road. Typically, passable by 2WD and smaller RV's. Total distance is 62 mi / 100 km to park.

- From Page, AZ: Take US-89 West to Hancock Road to Coral Pink Sand Dunes Road. Note that final leg from Hancock Road to park is on an unpaved gravel road, suitable for all vehicles.

What Makes Coral Pink Sand Dunes Special

- The cool color of the sand dunes, especially at dawn and dusk

- The ability to hike in a Zion like world with all the wonder but with less fellow tourists

- Knowing you can put that ATV you brought to great use

The first thing to note about this park is while the color is distinctly different from other sand dunes; it may not be the pink color you envisioned when you first pull up. The color is more of a sandstone red much of the time and requires the right soft and low but direct lighting to bring out the picture perfect coral color.

The elusive pink color aside, the park is a great stay over spot within the typical route of the Grand Circle. Here there are nice campgrounds, good restroom facilities and a playground of sand nearby. Perhaps the only downside if you aren't riding an ATV is all the ATV's in the dunes area. One definitely needs to be mindful of these high-speed vehicles in this multiuse area. That said, if you do have an ATV, the area allows exploration into canyons that are very much like Zion NP, but without all the people. For many locals, this is how they see Zion, by riding into the wilderness surrounding it.

There is one other minor but very cool feature of this park. It has an extensive collection of sand from all over the world. Each little jar is labeled with the sand's location. The collection, which takes up an entire wall in the visitor center, started as a ranger's hobby, but has grown considerably as tourists have sent in their local samples. It is quite possibly the largest collection of sand in the world and is worth checking out.

Hiking in Coral Pink Sand Dunes State Park

Coral Pink Sand Dunes Arch

Easy – (0.2 mi / 0.3 km), round trip, allow 15 minutes elev. Δ: 50 ft / 15 m, trailhead on Hancock Road

This is by no means the grandest arch you will see, but is a welcome surprise for a park whose primary feature is a set of

Coral Pink Sand Dunes After a Rain Shower

sand dunes. Getting to this arch is easy. At the turnoff from Hancock Road from Highway 89, mark your trip meter and drive 0.8 miles. Drive off the road on your right for about 150 yards, heading towards the sole obvious hoodoo. From here, get out and walk past this hoodoo using the ATV trail on the left and look for two rock outcroppings. Here you will find a small but definite arch.

Coral Pink Sand Dunes

Easy – (1.0 mi / 1.6 km), round trip, allow 1 - 2 hours, elev. Δ: a00 ft / 30 m, trailhead at campground

The dunes are in easy sight as you pull up and the trailhead is easy enough to find, however it is recommended to keep along the established route so as not to disturb the fragile flora. Like all dunes, walking in sand can be more tiring than the same distance on hard ground. Also, hiking to the tallest dune, at a 300 feet elevation gain from its base, will add to the time. Look for insect and animal tracks, as well as areas of "plant art", where tall grasses have left their marks in the sand by the prevailing winds.

The one caution with the dunes is that the area is shared with ATV's. Keep an eye out for fast moving visitors. The ATV's can be a bit loud, but they are also fun to watch from the tall dunes.

South Fork Indian Canyon

Easy – (1.0 mi / 1.6 km), round trip, allow 30 minutes, elev. Δ: 150 ft / 46 m, trailhead at end of South Fork Indian Canyon Road off Sand Spring Road

This trail leads to some truly amazing pictographs. Formed around 1200 BCE, this rock art was created using natural pigments versus a petroglyph, which are formed by actually carving into the rock. The pictographs are quite rare and sit behind a protective fence. Bring a zoom lens if you want great pictures. This trail requires a 4WD vehicle that can handle the aptly named Sand Spring Road.

Take Sand Spring Road from Hancock for about a mile through the edge of the dunes and then a little less than two miles up South Fork Indian Canyon to the obvious parking lot for the pictographs. In many ways, this is the gem of the park and not the only one of its kind (See Hell Dive Canyon below)

Hell Dive Canyon

Moderate – (6.6 mi / 10.6 km), round trip, allow 4 – 5 hours, elev. Δ: 580 ft / 177 m, trailhead on 4WD road west of Water Canyon

This is another set of pictographs that are farther to get to and not protected. Please do not touch these very fragile pieces of

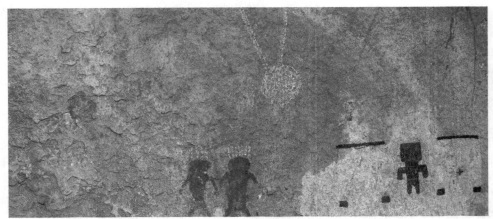

Pictographs at South Fork Indian Canyon

Still Life with Sand

history. Any contact with them can do permanent harm. To get here, head to the South Fork Indian Canyon road on Sand Spring Road and upon reaching it, stay right for about 0.8 miles, continuing on Sand Spring Road. At a fork in the road, head left and continue another 0.75 miles stopping when the road gets too rough for vehicles.

After parking, continue hiking down this road. The road becomes more trail and winds down to the bottom of Water Canyon and then climbs up a ridge to another intersection. Turn left here and continue in a southerly direction. Don't fret, as the trail veers to the northeast for a couple of miles, just make sure you don't take any right turns and you'll end up at Hell Dive Canyon. Continue into the alcove, where the pictographs can be found. Again, please be respectful in this area and don't touch the art.

Peek-a-Boo Slot Canyon

Easy – (0.7 mi / 1.1 km), round trip, allow 1 hour, trailhead described below

Peek-a-Boo or Red Canyon is not that long and is a very easy walk through a narrow red rock walled slot canyon with plenty of twists and turns (hence the nickname). While the trail itself isn't that long, the primary reason is the journey itself. It takes about 3 hours to get to the trailhead along deep sandy 4WD roads or optional ATV routes. The scenery along the way and the adventure getting there makes the slot canyon itself icing on the cake.

This canyon isn't in the park boundaries itself, but is very popular for ATV enthusiasts staying in Coral Pink Sand Dunes SP. From the park, head back to Highway 89 via Hancock Road and turn south. Look for the Best Friends Animal Society and make a left towards it. Total distance from the park to the sanctuary is 16 miles. Now on road 102M, make a left just before the animal sanctuary and continue on this deep sandy path for the canyon. Stay right at the first juncture where 102M splits for road 102. Continue on road 102 unless you can navigate very deep sand and want a bit more adventure, then take 102L, which is slightly shorter but has a nice steep hill to navigate. The slot canyon is at the end of the road.

Frontier Homestead State Park Museum

Frontier Homestead State Park Museum

Official Park Website: http://stateparks.utah.gov/parks/frontier-homestead//

Visitor Center: (435) 586-9290

Nearest Town with Amenities:

- The park is located in the town of Cedar City, UT

Getting There:

- From St George, UT: Take I-15 North. Total distance is 54 mi / 87 km to park

One of the best places to see Mormon pioneering history and artifacts, plus, some iron mining history, all in a clean mid-sized American town.

Frontier Homestead State Park Museum is located on Main Street in the pleasant town of Cedar, Utah. Cedar is one of those towns that started out through a defined purpose, in this case mining for iron. When the primary reason to be there ran dry, enough people stuck around anyway and figured out how to keep the town thriving. Today, Cedar is one of the larger towns in Utah and home to Southern Utah University and the Utah Shakespeare Festival.

Within the clean and well-organized society of Cedar is a museum holding a healthy amount of Mormon pioneer artifacts. The museum doesn't just hold little stuff; this place is large enough to showcase stagecoaches and horse buggies as well as the expected assortment of pioneer and ancestral inhabitant artifacts. The museum also tells the story of iron mining in the area under the direction of Brigham Young. Occasionally, the park holds frontier days, where folks dress up in period costumes and take part in pioneer tasks such as washing clothes by hand and roping cattle.

Cedar Breaks National Monument

Quick Facts

Official Park Website: http://www.nps.gov/cebr

Visitor Center: (435) 586-0787 ext. 4022

Park Accessibility:

- Okay for 2WD and RVs
- The park is open all year, however the road to park, UT-148, is closed after the first snowfall, usually in mid-November. The visitor center and campground are closed, but the park itself remains open during this time.

Experience Level:

- Family Friendly to Experienced Hiker

Camping in Park:

- Point Supreme Campground: 25 T/RV, drinking water, showers, restrooms, no hookups

Lodging and Dining in Park:

- None

Nearest Town with Amenities:

- Cedar City, UT is 27 mi / 43 km from park

Getting There:

- From St. George, UT: Take I-15 North to UT-14 East to UT-148. Total distance is 75 mi / 121 km to park entrance.

Sun Beam on Cedar Breaks

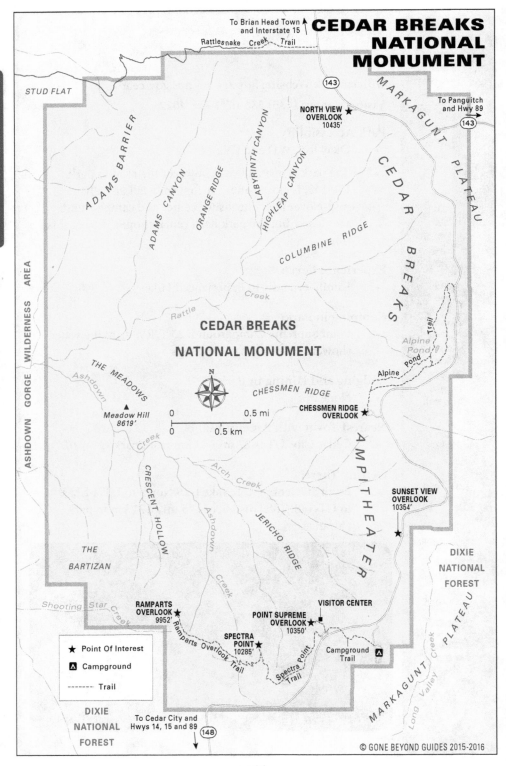

CEDAR BREAKS NATIONAL MONUMENT

To Brian Head Town and Interstate 15

Rattlesnake Creek Trail

STUD FLAT

143

To Panguitch and Hwy 89
143

NORTH VIEW OVERLOOK 10435'

ADAMS BARRIER

ADAMS CANYON

ORANGE RIDGE

LABYRINTH CANYON

HIGHLEAP CANYON

COLUMBINE RIDGE

CEDAR BREAKS

MARKAGUNT PLATEAU

Rattle Creek

CEDAR BREAKS NATIONAL MONUMENT

Alpine Pond Trail

Alpine Pond

ASHDOWN GORGE WILDERNESS AREA

THE MEADOWS

Ashdown

Meadow Hill 8619'

N

0   0.5 mi
0   0.5 km

CHESSMEN RIDGE

CHESSMEN RIDGE OVERLOOK

Creek

Arch Creek

CRESCENT HOLLOW

Ashdown Creek

JERICHO RIDGE

AMPITHEATER

SUNSET VIEW OVERLOOK 10354'

THE BARTIZAN

DIXIE NATIONAL FOREST

Shooting Star Creek

RAMPARTS OVERLOOK 9952'

Ramparts Overlook Trail

SPECTRA POINT 10285'

POINT SUPREME OVERLOOK 10350'

VISITOR CENTER

Spectra Point Trail

Campground Trail

MARKAGUNT PLATEAU

Long Valley Creek

★ Point Of Interest
🅰 Campground
------- Trail

DIXIE NATIONAL FOREST

To Cedar City and Hwys 14, 15 and 89
148

© GONE BEYOND GUIDES 2015-2016

Panoramic View of Cedar Breaks National Monument

What Makes Cedar Breaks Special

Cedar Breaks is kind of like the Pluto of the national monuments within the Grand Circle. At only 6,000 acres, it is debatable as to whether it is big enough to be a national monument, for one. Plus, it's kind of out of the way for folks doing the typical Grand Circle circuit. However, the biggest similarity is that upon closer inspection, the park is full of greatness and features you wouldn't expect to see.

Cedar Breaks is a natural amphitheater, similar to what you would expect to see at Bryce Canyon, but with colors that are darker and richer. The tones are deeper and more subdued at Cedar Breaks, something akin to Bryce Canyon's older, but wiser, fun-sized brother.

At 6,150 acres, the park is easily covered. There are only a handful of trails but most folks just come to lean up against the overlook and gaze out at "the breaks". For those that do stay at the campground and hike around, the reward is an intimate experience in the park coupled with a satisfying feeling you were able to "see it all".

Hiking in Cedar Breaks National Monument

The one constant for all of these hikes is the altitude. The elevation here is 10,000 plus feet, which can cause shortness of breath and will make an easy hike feel more strenuous. Also, there is less sun protection at this altitude, so make sure you lather up with sunscreen, and wear a hat and sunglasses. This is high enough in the mountains where odd parts get burned, such as the tips of your ears or the top of one's head for the hair challenged. Be prepared and as always, bring plenty of water and some clothing layers.

Campground Trail

Easy – (1.0 mi / 1.6 km), round trip, allow 30 minutes

This is a partially ADA compliant one mile walk that provide views of the amphitheater. The trail starts at the campground and ends at the visitor center. A great walk for kids wanting to get their junior badge programs or just to stretch the legs. The trail is dog friendly, as long as there is a leash involved.

Spectra Point & Ramparts Overlook Trail

Moderate – (4.0 mi / 6.4 km), round trip, allow 2 hours

This is the best hike to take for views of the Cedar Breaks amphitheater. The hike to Spectra Point Overlook is just one mile, which gives a more face on view of the amphitheater. If you do continue on the second mile of this there and back hike, you'll be treated by some ancient bristlecone pines.

Alpine Pond Nature Trail

Easy – (2.0 mi / 3.2 km), round trip, allow 1 hour

This is a great double loop through the high alpine woodlands of the Dixie National Forest. There are great views of the Cedar Breaks amphitheater, but often, sprays of native wildflowers will do a good job of trying to steal the show. There is also a small strand of ancient bristlecone pines to be seen along the way. The trail passes by the small Alpine Pond and is picked up from Chessman Ridge Overlook. To cut the hiking time in half, simply do not take the upper loop.

Rattlesnake Creek Trail

Strenuous – (19.6 mi / 31.5 km), round trip, full day hike or overnight backpacking trip

Tucked away at the northern entrance to the park is a really incredible hike. Here you are hiking at times amongst some of the same strata that formed the lower elevation red rock features, such as Zion NP, but at a much higher elevation. The result is a more forested, lush environment wrapping around the familiar rock layers

of the other parks. The other upsides here are pleasant summer weather and the sounds of the forest, such as the leaves of an Aspen grove. The one downside is the need for bug spray.

Most of the trail is managed by the U.S. Forest Service and is not maintained. There are spots where the trail is ill defined and will require some navigational and map reading skills. Bring a compass and a topo of the area if taking this trail. This trail has no easy exit and is essentially deep within the Dixie National Forest. Make sure you plan ahead and come prepared.

Rattlesnake Creek Trail drops a whopping 2,500 feet over four miles where it meets up with Ashdown Creek. From Ashdown Creek, you can either follow it upstream back into the canyons that make up the foot of the Cedar Breaks amphitheater or head downstream into the Ashdown Gorge Wilderness Area. Either direction is amazing; it is hard to make a recommendation of one over the other. Note that there is a fair amount of travel across privately owned land. Leave no trace and pass through with respect.

Thems the Breaks

Bryce Canyon National Park

Sunrise at Bryce Canyon

Quick Facts

Official Park Website: www.nps.gov/brca

Visitor Center: (435) 834-5322

Park Accessibility:
- Okay for 2WD and RVs
- Day and Overnight Use

Experience Level:
- Family Friendly to Experienced Hiker

Camping in Park:
- North Campground: 102 T/RV, drinking water, vault toilets, some pull thru sites, no hookups, dump station in summer, some sites reservable. Reserve at http://www.recreation.gov/
- Sunset Campground: 101 T/RV, drinking water, showers, vault toilets, no hookups, closed in winter, some sites reservable. Reserve at http://www.recreation.gov/

Lodging in Park:
- Bryce Canyon Lodge, Phone: (435) 834-8700

Dining in Park:
- Bryce Canyon Lodge offers breakfast, lunch and dinner. There is also a general store.

Nearest Town with Amenities:
- Bryce, UT is 1.5 mi / 2.4 km from park

Getting There:
- From St. George, UT: Take I-15N to UT-9 East, US-89 North and UT-12 East to UT-63 South 125 mi / 201 km to park entrance

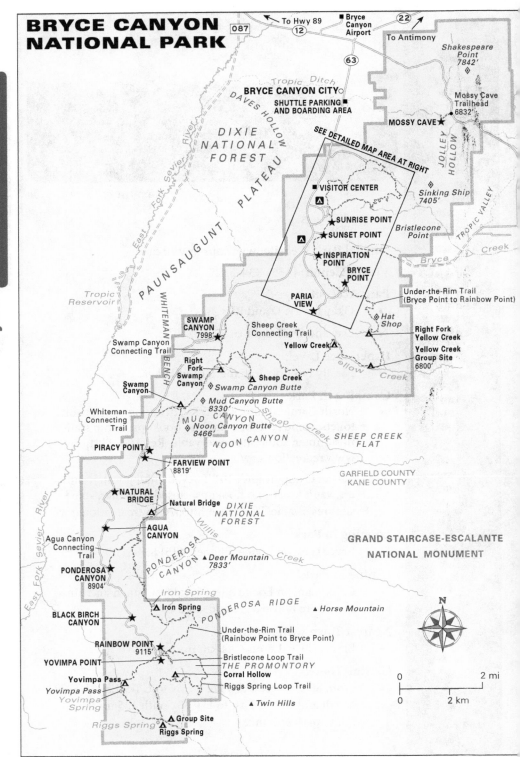

BRYCE CANYON
NATIONAL PARK

087

To Hwy 89
12

■ Bryce
Canyon
Airport

22

To Antimony

*Shakespeare
Point
7842'*

Tropic Ditch

63

BRYCE CANYON CITY ○

SHUTTLE PARKING
AND BOARDING AREA ■

*Mossy Cave
Trailhead
6832'*

MOSSY CAVE ★

D A V E S   H O L L O W

*D I X I E
N A T I O N A L
F O R E S T*

SEE DETAILED MAP AREA AT RIGHT

*Sinking Ship
7405'*

J O L L E Y   H O L L O W

■ **VISITOR CENTER**

★ **SUNRISE POINT**

★ **SUNSET POINT**

*Bristlecone
Point*

★ **INSPIRATION
POINT**

★ **BRYCE
POINT**

Under-the-Rim Trail
(Bryce Point to Rainbow Point)

★ **PARIA
VIEW**

Bryce   *Creek*

TROPIC VALLEY

P L A T E A U

P A U N S A U G U N T

*Tropic
Reservoir*

E a s t   F o r k   S e v i e r   R i v e r

**SWAMP
CANYON**
7998' ★

Sheep Creek
Connecting Trail

◇ *Hat
Shop*

**Right Fork
Yellow Creek**

Swamp Canyon
Connecting Trail

Yellow Creek △

**Yellow Creek
Group Site
6800'**

W H I T E M A N   B E N C H

**Right
Fork
Swamp
Canyon** △

△ **Sheep Creek**

Y e l l o w   *C r e e k*

**Swamp
Canyon**

◇ *Swamp Canyon Butte*

**Whiteman
Connecting
Trail**

△

◇ *Mud Canyon Butte
8330'*

M U D   C A N Y O N

◇ *Noon Canyon Butte
8466'*

S h e e p   *C r e e k*

*SHEEP CREEK
FLAT*

N O O N   C A N Y O N

PIRACY POINT ★

★ **FARVIEW POINT**
8819'

GARFIELD COUNTY
KANE COUNTY

★ **NATURAL
BRIDGE**

Natural Bridge

*D I X I E
N A T I O N A L
F O R E S T*

GRAND STAIRCASE-ESCALANTE

NATIONAL MONUMENT

★ **AGUA
CANYON**

**Agua Canyon
Connecting
Trail**

P O N D E R O S A

*Deer Mountain
7833'*

Creek

C A N Y O N

Willis

**PONDEROSA
CANYON**
8904' ★

Iron Spring

△ **Iron Spring**

▲ *Horse Mountain*

**BLACK BIRCH
CANYON**

P O N D E R O S A   R I D G E

E a s t   F o r k   S e v i e r   R i v e r

RAINBOW POINT
9115' ★

Under-the-Rim Trail
(Rainbow Point to Bryce Point)

YOVIMPA POINT ★

Bristlecone Loop Trail

THE PROMONTORY

Corral Hollow

Yovimpa Pass △

Riggs Spring Loop Trail

Yovimpa Pass
*Yovimpa
Spring*

▲ *Twin Hills*

Riggs Spring △ **Group Site**

△ **Riggs Spring**

N

0   2 mi

0   2 km

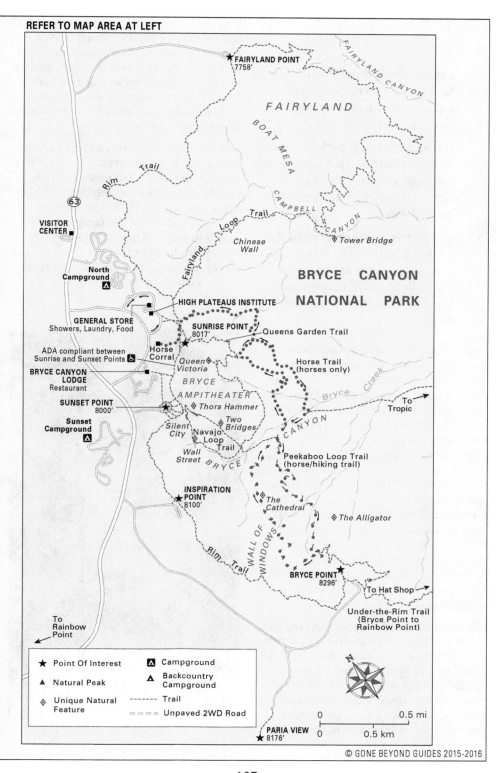

FAIRYLAND POINT
7758'

FAIRLAND CANYON

FAIRYLAND

BOAT MESA

CAMPBELL CANYON

63

VISITOR CENTER

Rim Trail

Fairyland Loop Trail

Chinese Wall

Tower Bridge

BRYCE CANYON

NATIONAL PARK

North Campground

HIGH PLATEAUS INSTITUTE

GENERAL STORE
Showers, Laundry, Food

SUNRISE POINT
8017'

Queens Garden Trail

Horse Corral

Queen Victoria

ADA compliant between
Sunrise and Sunset Points

Horse Trail
(horses only)

BRYCE CANYON LODGE
Restaurant

BRYCE AMPITHEATER

Bryce Creek

SUNSET POINT
8000'

Thors Hammer

To Tropic

Sunset Campground

Silent City

Navajo Loop Trail

Two Bridges

C A N Y O N

Wall Street

B R Y C E

Peekaboo Loop Trail
(horse/hiking trail)

INSPIRATION POINT
8100'

The Cathedral

The Alligator

WALL OF WINDOWS

Rim Trail

BRYCE POINT
8296'

To Hat Shop

To Rainbow Point

Under-the-Rim Trail
(Bryce Point to
Rainbow Point)

★ Point Of Interest

▲ Natural Peak

◇ Unique Natural Feature

🔺 Campground

🔺 Backcountry Campground

------ Trail

==== Unpaved 2WD Road

N

0   0.5 mi
0   0.5 km

PARIA VIEW
8176'

SOUTH CENTRAL UTAH

Bryce

What Makes Bryce Canyon Special

- Bryce Canyon is the template for Southwest scenery, holding the entire spectrum of desert colors in one place.

- It is an amusement park for hikers. There are tunnels, spires, hoodoos, (aka fairy chimneys) and pinnacles, all in an amphitheater of fruit colored rock.

- The park is considered one of the darkest night skies in the contiguous United States and has some of the farthest-reaching views during the day, up to 150 miles to the horizon.

Bryce Canyon is a wonderland of fluted rock and hoodoo pinnacles; hoodoos being thin tall spires of rock. Bryce Canyon has been the inspiration of movies, amusement park rides, desert-themed musicals, and art to the point of being the template for Southwest scenery. It is full of grandness and color all wrapped within a succession of massive natural amphitheaters. Bryce Canyon holds the entire spectrum of the colors of the desert in one place. From the top of the mesa, the view is breathtaking, grand, and colorful in so many hundreds of tones that it defies description. Light seems to emit from the canyon walls rather than reflect off of them, radiating to a glow at the tips of each hoodoo.

Hiking down inside Bryce amphitheater is like going on an amusement park ride. All journeys wind steadily downward followed by a delightful tramp up and down knolls, through man-carved tunnels and past massive hoodoos that form fragile spires. Once down below, the canyon floor is more whimsy and wonder with pines growing as tall as the spires, each turn worthy of another amazing shot. Hiking or horseback riding within Bryce is simply a fun experience. When you are done, you are a short shuttle ride back to Bryce Canyon Lodge, where they serve hearty meals in an atmosphere fashioned after the mid-1920s.

The other special quality of this national park is its elevation. Bryce Canyon NP sits at 9,000 feet (2,743 meters). From the mesa tops, one can see clear out 150 miles (241 km) to the horizon, an amazing view, and one of the farthest horizons visible in North America. The high elevation also brings snow in the winter and spring, capping the fruity-colored rocks with a sugary coating.

Douglas firs within the hoodoos

Hiking in Bryce Canyon NP

Mossy Cave

Easy – (0.8 mi / 1.3 km), round trip, allow 30 minutes, elev. Δ: 300 ft / 91 m, trailhead on Highway 12, 4 mi east of SR 63

A short hike that follows along a stream created by a man made diversion during the late 1800's by Mormon Pioneers. There are two spurs to this hike. The left spur ends at Mossy Cave, a large rocky overhang with a small waterfall that creates a nice mossy environment for plants. During the winter, look for icicle sheets created by the dripping waters, which are very cool and unusual. The right spur leads to a good-sized waterfall that also has been known to freeze completely during the winter.

Rim Trail

Easy – (0.9 mi / 1.5 km), one way, allow 1 hour, elev. Δ: 1,235 ft / 376 m, multiple trailheads along rim of Bryce Canyon

The Rim Trail from Sunrise Point to Sunset Point is flat and offers a leisurely way to take in the park. Pick up the trail from either point and follow the well-marked path. The Rim Trail does continue south from Sunset Point for a total of 5.5 miles (9.2km) one-way, but the trail from here has a lot of ups and downs and is considered strenuous.

Fairyland Loop

Strenuous – (8.0 mi /12.9 km), round trip, allow 5 hours, elev. Δ: 2,309 ft / 704 m, trailheads at Sunrise and Fairyland Points

Fairyland Loop is similar to Peekaboo but as it is a little longer, offers even more to the hiker. There is plenty to see on the trail, including China Wall, an impressively long wall of rock. You can also see a double arch with unique monolithic sentinels called Tower Bridge. Fairyland Loop is the least crowded trail of the popular trails at Bryce Canyon and is well worth it if you want to do a longer hike. Pick up the trail at Fairyland Point. The trail uses the Rim Trail to create a full loop.

Tower Bridge

Moderate – (3.0 mi / 4.8 km), round trip, allow 2 – 3 hours, elev. Δ: 950 ft / 290 m, trailhead at Sunrise Point

See Fairyland Loop for additional details. The trail starts at Sunrise Point and follows Fairyland Loop partially down until a juncture to a short spur trail to view Tower Bridge. Tower Bridge is a formation of two colorful hoodoos connected by a fragile layer of rock midway down the "towers". There is another natural bridge that can be seen in the same view. Head back up the same way you came down or continue onwards on the longer Fairyland Loop.

Queen's Garden Trail

Easy – (1.8 mi / 2.9 km), round trip, allow 2 hours, elev. Δ: 320 ft / 98 m, trailhead at Sunrise Point

Queen's Garden is 0.9 miles (1.4 km) down and the same distance back up. The trail is the least strenuous in terms of steepness compared to the other trails that head into the canyon, but it is by no means a flat trail. Picking up the Queen's Garden trail from Sunrise Point, hike down and wind your way through tunnels to the hoodoo called Queen Victoria and the surrounding rock formations that make up her garden. You can follow the trail back to the top, though many folks opt to combine this trail with the Navajo Trail to create a loop.

Peekaboo Trail

Strenuous – (5.5 mi / 8.8 km), round trip, allow 3 – 4 hours, elev. Δ: 1,555 ft / 473 m, trailhead at Bryce Point

Peekaboo is one of the best trails in Bryce Canyon. The loop is picked up from either Bryce Point or Sunset via the Navajo

Trail. The trail gives the hiker a sense of remoteness and a personal experience as you walk up and down gullies and past goblins, fins and rows of hoodoos. Every bend rewards the hiker with a different view of often-unimaginable rock shapes. You will find yourself a ways from the rim, in the heart of the amphitheater, which gives a better sense of grandness of Bryce Canyon. The loop can be done on its own or combined with Navajo or Queen's Garden Trails. Peekaboo is not terribly crowded, though it does get a fair amount of horse traffic.

Hat Shop Trail

Moderate – (4.0 mi /6.4 km), round trip, allow 2 - 3 hours, elev. Δ: 1,436 ft / 438 m, trailhead at Bryce Point

From the trailhead, descend via the Under the Rim Trail for 2 miles to a set of thin spired hoodoos with delicately balanced capstones defying gravity. The hike is a down and up, there and back hike. There are ample other Bryce Canyon type features along the way to the final destination.

Swamp Canyon

Moderate – (4.3 mi / 7.2 km), round trip, allow 2 - 3 hours, elev. Δ: 800 ft / 244 m, trailhead at Swamp Canyon Overlook

Swamp Canyon Trail starts at about the mid-point in the park, further south of the main amphitheaters. This loop trail offers a mixture of denser forest and the famous hoodoos. Unlike the endless stream of hikers coming down Navajo Trail, Swamp Canyon is definitely more intimate and may be a better option on crowded days.

Bristlecone Loop

Easy – (1.0 mi / 1.6 km), round trip, allow 30 minutes, elev. Δ: 195 ft / 59 m, trailhead at Rainbow Point, southern end of park

While most of the attention in Bryce is near the entrance of the park, the southern section of the park receives lets attention. Here the area contains more of a pleasant evergreen forest offering. Bristlecone Loop is a short hike in the southern section, displaying expansive views from 9,100 feet across a forested and green part of the state. As the trail name suggests, there are examples of the bristlecone pine, a gnarled and aged tree that can grow to 1,800 years here. The

Bryce Canyon in early spring

hike is pleasant and as the highest trail in the park, can be a little breathtaking for many reasons.

Riggs Spring Loop

Strenuous – (8.5 mi / 13.7 km), round trip, allow 4 – 5 hours, elev. Δ: 2,248 ft / 685 m, trailhead at Yovimpa Point

A very different side of Bryce, Riggs Spring is an ambling pleasant hike through fir, spruce, quaking aspens, and even ancient bristlecone pines. The hike is the southernmost trail in the park. As the trail's title suggests, there is a little spring in a shady setting. Do treat the water before using. This is a popular trail for overnight campers.

Along the floor of Bryce Canyon

Grand Staircase-Escalante National Monument

Quick Facts

Official Park Website: www.blm.gov/ut/st/en/fo/grand_stair-case-escalante.html

Visitor Center:

None in park, contact: BLM Kanab Headquarters, 669 South Highway 89A, Kanab, Utah 84741, Phone: (435) 644-1200

Park Accessibility:
- 2WD, 4WD recommended for most roads
- Day and Overnight Use

Experience Level:
- Primarily Experienced Hiker – Backcountry Hiker,
- Some trails Family Friendly - Casual Hiker

Camping in Park:
- No developed campground, backcountry camping okay with permit

Lodging and Dining in Park:
- None

Nearest Town with Amenities:
- Tropic, UT is 5 mi / 8 km from park

Getting There:
- From St. George, UT: Take UT-59 South and AZ-389 East 81 mi / 130 km to park entrance
- From Page, AZ: Take US-89 North 17 mi / 27 km to park entrance

Wahweap Hoodoo

What Makes Grand Staircase-Escalante Special

- Being nearly 1.9 million acres of pristine, diverse and multifaceted Utah desert, knowing you are hiking in the heart of the Colorado Plateau

- A remarkable and vast array of all manner of rarely seen arches, petroglyphs, hoodoos, canyons, slot canyons, lush riparian folds cut deep into rock walls and well, anything and everything that can be found in the Utah desert

- Roughly the size of three Rhode Islands and only two paved roads

A connection can be made with Glen Canyon National Recreation Area and the Grand Staircase-Escalante National Monument. The most obvious is that they are two very large parks siting right next to each other. Glen Canyon NRA protects a substantial portion of the Escalante River and its watershed, so they both share the last river to be named in the continental US. They both cover land that has been little disturbed, primarily because it is so rugged a country as to make it hard for the toils of man to penetrate. This is in fact why nearby Glen Canyon was filled with water, because there were no roads or towns to move. From the lens of the Bureau of Reclamation, there was nothing there.

It was only after the deed was done that folks realized there was something there after all, that this was a land worth protecting. Perhaps then, this is the deepest connection between the two parks. Within the profound disappointment by many of burying Glen Canyon with water, there was an acknowledgment that more must be done for those lands around it that are similar in spirit. To that, using the Antiq-

uities Act, President Bill Clinton created Grand Staircase-Escalante National Monument in 1996. It is the largest land area of all the US National Monuments.

While this act was applauded by environmentalists and can be seen as a sentiment in the right direction over what was done with Glen Canyon, it was not seen as positive by many of the residents of Utah. Clinton barely gave 24-hour notice to the Utah governor and state congress, giving them no time to react. The designation was attacked from many different angles and remains a sore subject with Utah residents.

Politics aside, Grand Staircase-Escalante is a massive, rugged, and pristine world. Entering it requires preparation, topo maps, and backcountry skills and for all of this preparation, its rewards are many. It is in many ways, the last frontier within the contiguous United States, where the meter of a person is on equal ground with the land.

Hiking Grand Staircase-Escalante NM

All of these hikes have dozens of variants. The routes described below are the most commonly traveled routes.

Lower Calf Creek Falls

Moderate – (5.9 mi / 9.5 km), round trip, allow 3 hours, elev. Δ: 250 ft / 76 m, trailhead at Calf Creek Campground

The trail starts by acknowledging the soft sand underneath your feet on a trail that seems nearly surreal in its beauty. The line of the trail cuts into a tree-lined oasis as the canyon floor meets with massive blocks of darkly streaked walls of Navajo Sandstone that tower above on each side. The hike up has to be seen to be believed. Look for numerous cliff dwelling ruins tucked into alcoves as well as alien looking humanoid petroglyphs.

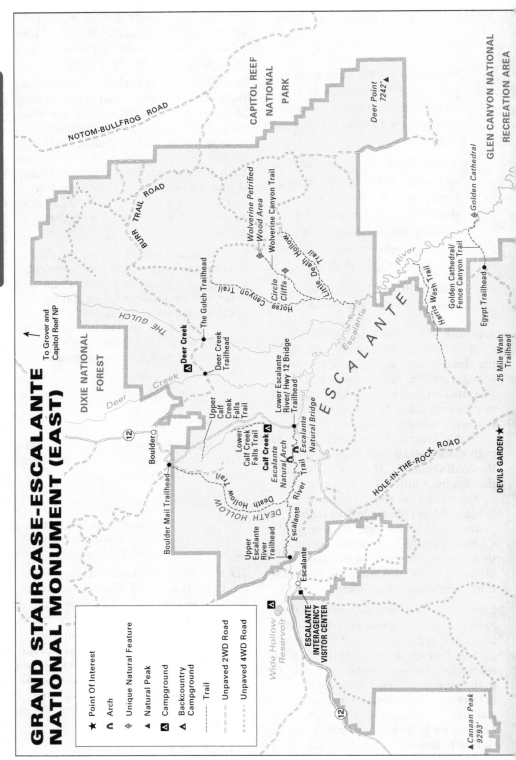

GRAND STAIRCASE-ESCALANTE
NATIONAL MONUMENT (EAST)

★ Point Of Interest

∩ Arch

◈ Unique Natural Feature

▲ Natural Peak

◭ Campground

▲ Backcountry Campground

- - - - - Trail

═ ═ ═ Unpaved 2WD Road

▪▪▪▪▪ Unpaved 4WD Road

CAPITOL REEF NATIONAL PARK

GLEN CANYON NATIONAL RECREATION AREA

NOTOM-BULLFROG ROAD

Deer Point 7242'

Golden Cathedral

BURR TRAIL ROAD

Wolverine Petrified Wood Area

Wolverine Canyon Trail

Little Death Hollow Trail

Horse Canyon Trail

Circle Cliffs

River

THE GULCH

The Gulch Trailhead

DIXIE NATIONAL FOREST

To Grover and Capitol Reef NP

Golden Cathedral/ Fence Canyon Trail

Harris Wash Trail

Egypt Trailhead

ESCALANTE

Escalante

Deer Creek

Deer Creek

Deer Creek Trailhead

Upper Calf Creek Falls Trail

Lower Escalante River/Hwy 12 Bridge Trailhead

25 Mile Wash Trailhead

(12)

Boulder

Lower Calf Creek Falls Trail

Calf Creek

Escalante Natural Arch

Escalante Natural Bridge

Boulder Mail Trailhead

DEATH HOLLOW

Death Hollow Trail

Escalante River Trail

Upper Escalante River Trailhead

HOLE-IN-THE-ROCK ROAD

DEVILS GARDEN ★

Escalante

ESCALANTE INTERAGENCY VISITOR CENTER

Wide Hollow Reservoir

(12)

▲ Canaan Peak 9293'

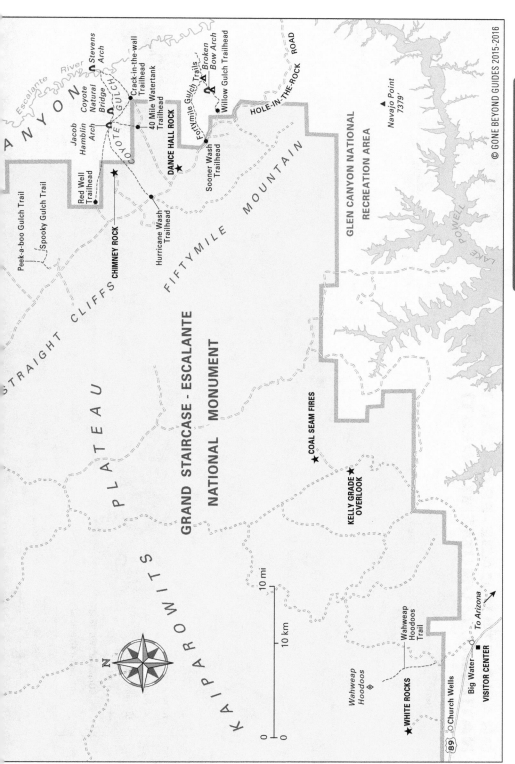

SOUTH CENTRAL UTAH

Grand Staircase-Escalante

Escalante River

A N Y O N

Stevens Arch

Coyote Natural Bridge

Jacob Hamblin Arch

COYOTE GULCH

★ Red Well Trailhead

Peek-a-boo Gulch Trail

Spooky Gulch Trail

★ CHIMNEY ROCK

Crack-in-the-wall Trailhead

40 Mile Watertank Trailhead

DANCE HALL ROCK ★

Fortymile Gulch Trails

Broken Bow Arch

Willow Gulch Trailhead

Sooner Wash Trailhead

HOLE-IN-THE-ROCK ROAD

Hurricane Wash Trailhead

FIFTYMILE MOUNTAIN

STRAIGHT CLIFFS

P L A T E A U

GRAND STAIRCASE - ESCALANTE
NATIONAL MONUMENT

GLEN CANYON NATIONAL
RECREATION AREA

Navajo Point
7379'

LAKE POWELL

★ COAL SEAM FIRES

★ KELLY GRADE OVERLOOK

K A I P A R O W I T S

N

10 mi

10 km

Wahweap Hoodoos Trail

Wahweap Hoodoos

★ WHITE ROCKS

Church Wells

Big Water

VISITOR CENTER

To Arizona

89

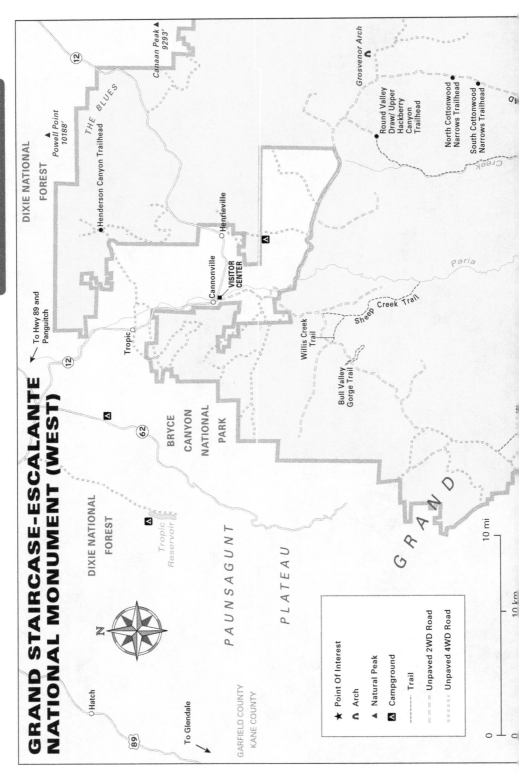

GRAND STAIRCASE-ESCALANTE
NATIONAL MONUMENT (WEST)

To Glendale

To Hatch

GARFIELD COUNTY
KANE COUNTY

N

DIXIE NATIONAL
FOREST

Tropic
Reservoir

PAUNSAGUNT

PLATEAU

BRYCE
CANYON
NATIONAL
PARK

Tropic

To Hwy 89 and
Panguitch

DIXIE NATIONAL
FOREST

THE BLUES

Powell Point
10188'

Canaan Peak
9293'

Henderson Canyon Trailhead

Henrieville

Cannonville

VISITOR
CENTER

Paria

Willis Creek
Trail

Sheep Creek Trail

Bull Valley
Gorge Trail

G R A N D

Creek

Grosvenor Arch

Round Valley
Draw/Upper
Hackberry
Canyon
Trailhead

North Cottonwood
Narrows Trailhead

South Cottonwood
Narrows Trailhead

Legend:
★ Point Of Interest
∩ Arch
▲ Natural Peak
△ Campground
------- Trail
▭▭▭ Unpaved 2WD Road
▭▭▭ Unpaved 4WD Road

10 mi

10 km

0

136

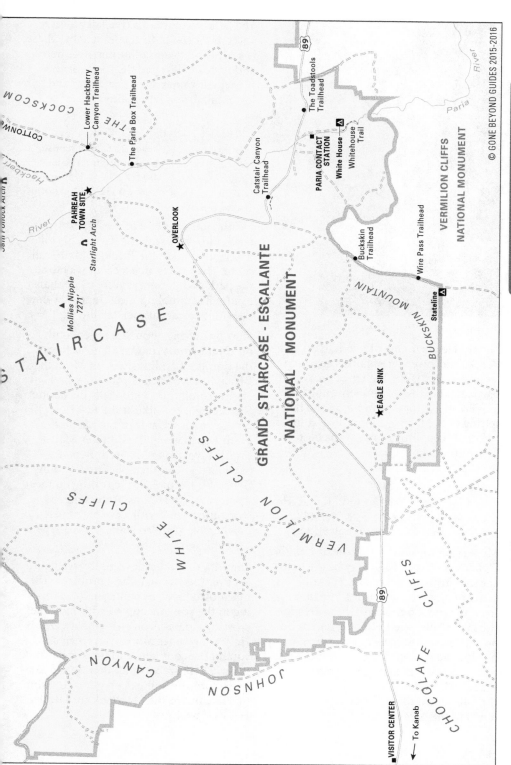

Grand Staircase-Escalante

COTTONWOOD

THE COCKSCOMB

Lower Hackberry Canyon Trailhead

The Paria Box Trailhead

Hackberry

River

San Fonock Arch

PAHREAH TOWN SITE

Starlight Arch

OVERLOOK

Mollies Nipple 7271'

STAIRCASE

GRAND STAIRCASE - ESCALANTE NATIONAL MONUMENT

Catstair Canyon Trailhead

The Toadstools Trailhead

Paria

River

PARIA CONTACT STATION

White House

Whitehouse Trail

VERMILION CLIFFS NATIONAL MONUMENT

Buckskin Trailhead

Wire Pass Trailhead

BUCKSKIN MOUNTAIN

Stateline

EAGLE SINK

VERMILION CLIFFS

WHITE CLIFFS

JOHNSON CANYON

89

CHOCOLATE CLIFFS

VISITOR CENTER

To Kanab

89

Lower Calf Creek Falls

The falls are more of a free fall of water and are shorter at 88 feet in height. There is a nice and deep swimming hole here and typically less people. As far as the hike quality goes, both the upper and lower falls are worth seeing.

Death Hollow

Strenuous – (14.0 mi / 22.5 km), round trip, full day trip or overnight backpacking trip, elev. Δ: 600 ft / 183 m, trailhead 24 mi from Escalante on Hell's Backbone Road north

Death Hollow is one of the largest tributaries into the Escalante River. This hike description takes the Boulder Mail Trail route. The hike is an excellent way to see the park and doesn't require more than minimal scrambling. Best done as a shuttle with two cars at each trailhead.

Start by driving about 3.8 miles south on UT 12 from Anasazi State Park to the Boulder Landing Strip on McGath Bench Road, which is your very first left after turning right onto Hells Backbone Road. Begin the hike at the junction on the northeast side of the McGath Point Bench along the Boulder Mail Trail. Travel along McGrath Bench, Sand Creek, and then Slickrock Saddle Bench for about 3.5 miles until you meet up with Death Hollow. Access here is straightforward, with a couple of places where you'll need some Class 3 type scrambling.

The trail leads to one of two falls on Calf Creek. The lower set of falls is spectacular and in fact is the higher of the two at 130 feet. There is a nice swimming hole to relax in as you take in the grotto like setting of the falls, greenery, and colored layers of rock. This is one of the best-known trails in the park.

Upper Calf Creek Falls

Strenuous – (2.2 mi / 3.5 km), round trip, allow 1 – 2 hours, elev. Δ: 505 ft / 154 m, trailhead on SR 12, east of milepost 81

More strenuous but no less beautiful, the Upper Calf Creek Falls may be the better choice during peak season. The trail starts on the west side UT 12 further up from the more popular parking area for the lower falls. The trailhead, near milepost 81, does not have a signpost. Start by heading downslope steeply on slickrock, using cairns as guides. The route descends 600 feet to the rim overlooking the falls. From there, follow the route down to the base of the falls.

Once in, the water flows pretty well, but is never too strong to be a problem. The hike down involves a mixture of walking in the stream coupled with multiple crossings to paths on either bank. Death Hollow becomes more overgrown as you hit the confluence to the Escalante River. There are lots of little side canyons to explore and some deep pools to swim in. Hike out to the Overlook for Death Hollow Parking Area.

Upper Escalante River

Moderate to Strenuous – (13.0 mi / 20.9 km), one-way, elev. Δ: 500 ft / 152 m, trailhead along river at Escalante, UT

There aren't many hikes in the world where you can literally close the door to your hotel room and just take a long walk down a river canyon and when you are done, get picked up with ease right from the highway. This hike exists and it is one of the gems of the Southwest in terms of beauty. It meanders gently downstream and passes arches and natural bridges, thick wonderful canyon walls, and even some swimming holes.

First off, for hikers, this description can be followed during the dry season when the river is low enough to wade down. During the wet season, the route is more suitable for river rafting, inner tubing, and kayaking.

The hike starts just about anywhere within the town of Escalante where you can access the river. If you want to reduce the amount of river wading whilst in town, find your way to the Pine Creek Escalante River Confluence at the northeast end of town. Not much in the way of parking here, but you'll soon be in the thick of the riparian desert wilderness from here.

Once inside the canyon, the river meanders almost as a rule, snaking along one bend after the other, giving to the curious the wonder of what could be around the next bend. The meanders allow for constantly changing views as well. One of the first notable formations to see is the Escalante Natural Arch, which sits high up on the south wall and is super easy to miss. Look for it after the confluence with Sand Creek. Less than 0.5 miles further on is Escalante Natural Bridge, a humbling and beautiful sight as well as the largest formation in the park. The bridge also marks the home stretch of the hike. Look for the UT 12 Bridge and your ride to home base back in Escalante. Your ride will pass by the Kiva Koffeehouse, which serves espressos seasonally from April to October in a very nice rustic building with great views.

Escalante Natural Bridge

Easy – (3.5 mi / 5.6 km), round trip, allow 2 hours, elev. Δ: 100 ft / 30 m, trailhead at Highway 12 bridge over Escalante River

For those that don't have the time to hike downstream from the town of Escalante, it is possible to see the Escalante Natural Bridge and do a bit of river trail hiking coming from the UT 12 Bridge that crosses over the Escalante River. Look for signs that indicate Escalante River trailhead access about 14 miles from the town of Escalante, heading south. The Escalante Natural Arch is about 0.5 miles further upstream (add 1.0 mile to your round trip distance).

Fortymile and Willow Gulch Loop

Moderate – (11.0 mi / 17.7 km), round trip, allow 6 hours, elev. Δ: 540 ft / 165 m, trailhead at Sooner Wash Trailhead off Hole in the Rock Road

Narrow canyons, bold rock faces, and a maze of seemingly endless hiking possibilities, this is Fortymile and Willow Gulch. There are many ways to explore this area, but in this description, the route starts at Sooner Wash Trailhead. Folks can start out at the adjacent Dance Hall Rock Campsite and check out the cool looking Sooner Rocks. The trailhead and the campsite are off Hole in the Rock Road. Note that this hike has spots where you will need to wade through waterholes and depending on water levels, may even require some swimming to get past the water obstacles.

From Sooner Wash Trailhead hike for 1.5 miles into the confluence of Sooner Wash and Fortymile Gulch. This portion will have some areas that require wading through canyon water pockets.

Continue for several miles to the Willow Gulch confluence. Here you can keep going down Fortymile Gulch as it meets up with Lake Powell, however the going is muddier. This description heads up Willow Gulch, which avoids the mucky bits and takes the hiker to Broken Bow Arch, which is about 0.5 miles up Willow Gulch from the confluence.

Devils Garden at night

Willow Gulch is definitely the more pristine of the two choices at the juncture. To exit, hike up any of the three main streams that feed the tributary. The northernmost stream is the most convenient of the three as it passes by a parking area near Hole in the Rock Road. Either hike back to your car from here or be thankful you brought two cars and parked one at the exit site. If you do have a second car, the total trip is 8.2 miles.

Hole in the Rock Trail

Strenuous – (1.0 mi / 1.6 km), round trip, allow 1 hour, elev. Δ: 600 ft / 182 m, trailhead on Highway 12 , just southeast of Escalante

Early Mormon pioneers used this steep but marginally passable draw as the route down to the Colorado River. The first thing one thinks when coming to the rim of the steep and narrow gully is something along the lines of, "They took their wagons and animals down that??"

The pioneers blasted the crevice to make it wide enough for wagons.

Today, this old supply route can be hiked down to what is now Lake Powell. It's very steep and very rocky, but fortunately only about a half mile. The trail has a plaque at the bottom commemorating the tenacity of these early settlers.

Devils Garden

Easy – (0.5 mi / 0.8 km), round trip, allow 30 – 60 minutes, elev. Δ: 10 ft / 3 m, trailhead on Hole in the Rock Road

This is a great family trail just off the Hole in the Rock Road. Here there be hoodoos and arches, of all manner of shapes and sizes, oddly misshapen things, every last one of them. To get to this garden of the devil himself, simply head east five miles on UT 12 from Escalante to the unpaved Hole in the Rock Road, which is suitable for 2WD vehicles in dry weather. Another 13 miles on Hole in the Rock takes you to a signed turnoff to Devils Garden. Park and roam around. There are picnic tables, BBQ grills and a pit toilet here, making this a nice lunch spot. This is a great place to make a deal.

Golden Cathedral

Moderate – (9.5 mi / 15.3 km), round trip, allow 5 - 6 hours, elev. Δ: 1,260 ft / 384 m, trailhead in Egypt area off Hole in the Rock Road

Golden Cathedral is a strikingly beautiful and unworldly set of three arches. Together they form a line of holes that resemble a massive rock spine. There is great light play here, that helps give the formation its name. The hike requires some decent navigational skill, winding down Fence Canyon into the confluence of Neon Canyon and the Escalante River.

Take Hole in the Rock Road to Egypt Bench Road and follow it for 9.9 miles. High clearance vehicles recommended here, as there are several washes to cross. At 2.9 miles, you will pass the trailhead for Twentyfive Mile Wash. At 6.4 miles, the road will turn sharply right into a wash and one mile later, you will need to navigate up a short but rocky and steep incline. Take the fork at 9.3 miles and turn right, parking the car at the Egypt trailhead after 9.9 miles.

From here, while there isn't much in the way of official trail, there are plenty of cairns to follow. You are at the highest point in the hike and will now drop down into Fence Canyon. Keep to the left of Fence Canyon as you come to it in order to head down into the wash and the confluence of the Escalante River and Fence Canyon. Also, be sure to note the route as you head down so you can find it on your way back.

From here, pull out your water shoes and follow the Escalante River downstream one-mile south from the confluence with Fence Canyon to Neon Canyon, which is the first side canyon on your left.

Head up Neon Canyon for another 0.9 miles to Golden Cathedral. This last stretch and the triptych of arches is serene and majestic and worth the trek to get there. Heading further up Neon Canyon requires ropes and technical skills.

Peek-a-Boo Gulch

Moderate – (2.0 mi / 3.2 km), round trip, allow 1 – 2 hours, elev. Δ: 100 ft / 30 m, trailhead at Dry Fork area off Hole in the Rock Road

Peek-a-Boo is a really fun little slot canyon. The trailhead is 26 miles northeast on Hole in the Rock Road and then take Dry Fork Turnoff, staying left. Take the short hike from Dry Fork Overlook to the bottom of Dry Fork. Peek-a-Boo is just ahead to the north. Dry Fork Road is barely passable by 2WD vehicles, but is better for high clearance rigs.

What makes this slot canyon fun is all of the little scramble puzzles that need to be figured out. Lots of little dry falls and chockstones. Finding the right route

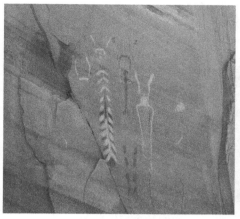

In Coyote Gulch

up the dry fall or figuring out whether to go under the big rock in the way or climb over it makes this a fun canyon to solve. A great hike for kids as none of the scrambling is that technical, though smaller children may need the occasional boost up.

The slot canyon is very narrow, though Spooky Gulch, which is typically combined with a hike through Peek-a-Boo, makes this gulch seem wide and spacious by comparison. Most folks scramble up Peek-a-Boo and then cross over and head into Spooky Gulch.

To combine the two slot canyons and make it a loop hike, scramble up Peek-a-Boo and then head overland through sandy red open terrain to the wide dry wash of Spooky Gulch. From there, head through Spooky back to Dry Fork and your car. This loop is 3.5 miles total.

Spooky Gulch

Moderate – (3.2 mi / 5.1 km), round trip, allow 2 -3 hours, elev. Δ: 100 ft / 30 m, trailhead at Dry Fork area off Hole in the Rock Road

Spooky Gulch is another short slot canyon that can be done alone or by combining with Peek-a-Boo Gulch. To get to Spooky Gulch, take the same route as to Peek-a-Boo from the Dry Fork Road.

141

Spooky Gulch is very different from Peek-a-Boo, though they are right next to each other. Whereas Peek-a-Boo is essentially a fun series of scramble puzzles to solve, Spooky is an extremely thin and deep slot canyon. It is so narrow that in some places there is only room for one person at time to pass. The canyon can make it feel like you are being compressed by the walls and some folks hit the narrow section at first thinking that it is too narrow to enter. You can and it does go all the way through, but it is definitely more of a spooky slot canyon than a soulful one. Those that are claustrophobic might want to take a pass on this one.

Coyote Gulch

Strenuous – (11.5 mi / 18.5 km), round trip, allow 5 - 6 hours or two-night backpacking trip, elev. Δ: 970 ft / 296 m, trailhead, see below

Coyote Gulch offers incredible scenery and some unique formations along the way. The trek is strenuous and it is recommended to make this a two-day jaunt. There is one section, Crack-in-the-Wall, that makes an argument for the day hike option if you don't have two days to spare, simply because it such an amazing and cool way to get down a cliff face.

The hike starts at some water tanks located 4.4 miles up Fortymile Ridge Road after coming from Hole-in-the-Rock Road in Escalante. The trail climbs up to Crack-in-the-Wall (or Crack-in-the-Rock), which is the first obstacle to surmount. The crack in question is a massive section of sandstone cliff that has broken off from the main section and moved outwards just enough for a grown person to shimmy in between. For the uninitiated, this may sound terrifying but it is easier than it may sound. Start by following the cairns to the very edge of the cliff and head right and down to what looks like the end of the cliff. Here you will find a crack that you shimmy in between to work to the canyon floor.

There are two areas of exposure, but for the most part, the crack is safe and is an exhilarating means of getting down to the river and upstream from there. If you are backpacking, it is recommended to lower your packs down by rope.

The scenery is amazing throughout and Coyote Gulch itself does not disappoint. Here one can fine one of the largest arches in the United States, Stevens Arch, standing 160 feet tall and spanning 225 feet. This is a hulk of an arch, simply massive. Then there is Coyote Bridge, a very picturesque natural bridge with water flowing underneath it year round.

Finally, there is Jacob Hamblin Arch, which marks the exit point for the hike. This is for some the hardest part of the hike. Hikers must be able to navigate up a 100-foot section of very steep slickrock to exit onto Fortymile Ridge. If you have anyone in the group that has doubts about this section, have the leader ascend and drop a rope down to aid in the climb up. This section is very exposed and at 45 degrees, is very steep. Once at the top of the ridge, head back to the water tanks and your vehicle.

Little Death Hollow

Easy – (16.0 mi / 25.7 km), round trip, full day or backpacking trip, elev. Δ: 600 ft / 183 m, trailhead: see description below

Grand Staircase has not one but two areas named Death Hollow. This hike refers to the beautiful slot canyon of Little Death Hollow. No one is sure what the relationship is between the Hollows, father and son perhaps? Whatever the connection, you can discuss this as you travel through this remote canyon. Little Death Hollow is popular for its long and narrow slot canyon, which is for the most part, obstacle free. The hike heads into the canyon and slot canyon further up with a turnaround point at the confluence with Horse Canyon. As with all hikes that involve narrow slot canyons,

Little Death Hollow Slot Canyon

be well aware of the weather to avoid being caught in a flash flood.

Little Death Hollow is in a more remote and generally less accessible part of the park, east of UT 12. To get there drive 19 miles east from Boulder, UT along Burr Trail Road and then turn right and head south on the unpaved Wolverine Loop Road. From this junction you will see a signpost indicating that the trailhead for Little Death Hollow is 12 miles on. This road is recommended for high clearance vehicles and even then, is impassable when wet. The main problem areas are at the two streambed crossings, Horse Canyon and Wolverine Creek. It will look level and inviting at the junction, but the road has some steep and sandy parts that are designed by nature to get 2WD cars stuck.

Once the turnoff for Wolverine Loop Road is found, take the right junction, heading counter-clockwise around the loop. This will allow for checking out the Wolverine Petrified Wood Natural Area, which is as amazing as Petrified Forest

National Park, but without the crowds. Be courteous to all of the generations ahead of you and refrain from picking up any pieces. From the petrified wood area, continue on the loop. It will cut east and then south into a valley before the entrance to Little Death Hollow. As remote as this is, there is a trail register and official trailhead. If you gotten this far, "Woot!" Let the hiking begin.

The canyon of Little Death Hollow starts out wide at first with cattle tracks paralleling the trail at first. The canyon continues to narrow and at some point, you realize you are in the slot canyon. In some sections, the canyon is just two feet wide and the water cut sandstone produces multiple lines horizontal to the ground. Depending on the season, there are pools of standing water that need to be crossed. These can be more like quicksand at times, especially after a rainstorm, so be careful.

The route ends at the confluence with Horse Canyon. From here, you can continue downstream to the Escalante River (about 3 miles further on) or head upstream to Wolverine Creek. If you take the upstream route, you can head up Wolverine Creek and hike the length of it to the head of the canyon, which sits just below the Wolverine Petrified Wood Natural Area. This adds another 1.5 miles to the hike, but gives a completely different view on the way back. Wolverine Creek is the first canyon on the right as you head up Horse Canyon. There is one junction as you head up Wolverine, stay to the right to exit closer to the Little Death Hollow Trailhead.

Cottonwood Canyon Road
Easy to Strenuous – Distance Varies

Cottonwood Road loosely follows the Paria River through Grand Staircase-Escalante NM from Highway 89 to Cannonville 46 miles to the north. The road offers incredible scenery, with views of

SOUTH CENTRAL UTAH Grand Staircase-Escalante

143

Cottonwood Canyon Road

river canyons, fins, and barren alien lands that look as if not of this planet. The road is impassable when wet, but is otherwise a great way to see a decent cross section of the park. Along the stretch are seemingly endless hiking opportunities. Sites to explore include Hackberry Canyon, Yellow Mountain, Cottonwood Canyon Narrows, the Cockscomb, and Grosvenor Arch.

The road also leads to Kodachrome State Park. Cottonwood Canyon Road can be picked up near milepost 18 on Highway 89 or from Kodachrome State Park Road.

Round Valley Draw

Moderate – (4.3 mi / 6.9 km), round trip, allow 2 -3 hours, elev. Δ: 400 ft / 122 m, trailhead is 1.5 miles on Rush Beds Road

Off Cottonwood Canyon Road and close to Grosvenor Arch is another slot canyon called Round Valley Draw. This slot canyon has some beautiful striations and in some areas is covered by suspended rock fall held in place above by the canyon walls.

From the north end of Cottonwood Canyon Road, drive south, then east for 14 miles. There is a signed spur road that heads south and winds up the Round Valley Wash to the mouth of the slot canyon. Off roaders can take the creek bed right up to the mouth, use good judgment on when to get out and start hiking otherwise.

From here, descend into the slot from the mesa top. There is a tree stump at the initial descent point to help navigate down into the slot. The total elevation down is about 15 feet. When the canyon opens up again, climb out back onto the mesa and hike out the way you came. For a longer journey, continue down the draw to Hackberry Creek. Round trip from Hackberry Creek is 5.5 miles.

Note that this slot canyon has contained obstacles that are best navigated with canyoneering skill and equipment (a good length of rope). There is one boulder that can sometimes be navigated by going under while at other times, the 15-foot obstacle requires a rope or good free climbing skills.

Paria Rimrocks Trail

Moderate – (1.5 mi / 2.4 km), round trip, allow 30 minutes, elev. Δ: 100 ft / 30 m, trailhead: see description below

Some of the coolest rock features in the area; Paria Rimrocks has to be seen to be believed. The trail follows a wash and then cairns to a goblin and hoodoo garden. The area is laden with hoodoos and toadstools, including one known as ET

Paria Rimrocks - Toadstool Trail

(aka Red Toadstool). Bring your camera; this is one of the more amazing hikes in the area.

Paria Rimrocks are near Highway 89 near mile marker 19. If driving north from Glen Canyon Dam, there will be a dirt parking area on the right just past the marker. There are maps available at the Grand Staircase-Escalante NM Visitor Center.

Harris Wash

Moderate – (21.2 mi / 34.1 km), round trip, full day or backpacking trip, elev. Δ: 700 ft / 213 m, trailhead is 4.5 mi south of Escalante on Hole-in-the-Rock Road

Harris Wash is one of the more accessible areas of Grand Staircase-Escalante NM and is also one of the most rewarding. It is the longest tributary of the Escalante River and can be done in full to the river as an overnight backpacking trip or as a day hike, going as far one's spirit of adventure takes them. There are many tributaries to explore, including Zebra and Tunnel Slot canyons, making this one of those hikes where there is seemingly something new around every bend.

Upper Harris Wash offers little in terms of scenery. The beginning of the route is as a small child, shy at first and not showing its true self until deeper into the draw. Big Horn Canyon joins from the north about 1.8 miles in and holds many interesting branches and narrow sections to explore.

At 4.3 miles one reaches Zebra Slot canyon, known for its orange sandstone layers striped with thin bands

of white. This tributary is well worth exploring. There are some dryfall obstacles to overcome as well as water filled pools, especially in wet weather.

Going downstream in Harris Wash another mile from Zebra Slot canyon leads to Tunnel Slot canyon. This is a short and cave like section, that follows for about 50 yards with high cliff walls surrounding a narrow passage. One typically will need to wade or even swim through a deep pool at start. The canyon then opens up to a scene of riparian brush and trees. The tunnel is just a few minutes from the main canyon.

There is another tributary about a half mile further downstream, containing serene vistas, several small springs and a simply pleasant vibe all around. Further down is Red Breaks, a seldom explored side canyon with deep passages and some shallow slot canyons. Opposite Red Breaks is the Harris Wash trailhead, used as a short cut to Escalante River from Halfway Hollow. It is possible to take Halfway Hollow back to Hole-in-the-Rock Road and north 3.5 miles to your car.

Harris Wash

Photo Attributes

Grand Canyon National Park

- Canyon Mid Day, by Realbrvhrt, CC-BY-SA-3.0-migrated
- Grand Canyon Panorama, by Roger Bolsius, CC-BY-SA-3.0
- North Rim, by Scott Catron, CC-BY-SA-3.0-migrated
- Grand Canyon North, by Khlnmusa, CC-BY-SA-3.0
- Lower Ribbon Falls, by Kkaufman11, PD-self
- South of Point Imperial, by NPS, PD US Government
- Ewe in Canyon, by Ronthemon2, PD-self
- Grand Canyon Geology, by NPS, PD-USGov
- A Grand Canyon Dory maneuvers through Hance Rapid, NPS Photo by Kristen M. Caldon, PD US NPS
- Grand Canyon panorama, by chensiyuan, CCBY-SA-3.0,2.5,2.0,1.0
- Desert View Watchtower, by Kevin A. Trostle, CC-BY-SA-3.0
- Skywalk, by Jonas.tesch, CC-BY-SA-3.0

Pipe Springs National Monument

- Pipe Spring, by Nikater, PD-self
- Pipe Spring, by John Fowler, CC-BY-2.0

Southwest Utah

- Kolob Canyons, by Gmhatfield, CC-Zero

Snow Canyon State Park

- Snow Canyon SP, by AJA, CC-BY-SA-4.0
- Snow Canyon SP, by Óðinn, CC-BY-SA-2.5-CA

Gunlock State Park

- Gunlock SP, by NPS, PD US NPS

Zion National Park

- Zion Narrows, by Jon Sullivan, PD-author
- Sunrise in Zion Canyon, by Stuart Seeger, CC-BY-2.0
- Waterfall at Emerald Pools Trail, by Stuart Seeger, CC-BY-2.0
- Climbing up Angels Landing, by Alex Proimos, CC-BY-2.0
- Zion Colors, by NPS, PD US NPS
- Into the Narrows, by Ada Be, CC-BY-2.0
- West Temple, by Ranger Bryanna Plog, PD US NPS
- Subway, by God of War, CC-BY-3.0
- Kolob Canyons, by Gmhatfield, CC-Zero
- Kolob Arch, by NPS, PD US NPS

Quail Creek State Park

- Quail Creek Reservoir, by Fredlyfish4, CC-BY-SA-3.0

Sand Hollow State Park

- Sand Hollow, by Dylan Duvergé, CC-BY-2.0

Coral Pink Sand Dunes SP

- Coral Pink Sand Dunes, by Eric Henze, copyright Gone Beyond Guides
- Sunrise in Zion Canyon, by Nandaro, CC-BY-SA-3.0
- Coral Pink Sand Dunes, by Eric Henze, copyright Gone Beyond Guides
- Coral Pink Sand Dunes, by Eric Henze, copyright Gone Beyond Guides

Frontier Homestead SP Museum

- Front of Frontier Museum SP, by NPS, PD US NPS

Cedar Breaks NM

- Cedar Breaks, by Michael Gäbler, CC-BY-3.0
- Cedar Breaks Panorama, by LeavXC, CC-BY-SA-3.0
- Cedar Breaks, by LeavXC, CC-BY-SA-3.0

Bryce Canyon National Park

- Bryce at Sunrise, by Eric Henze, Copyright Gone Beyond Guides
- Tree in canyon, by unknown, CC-BY-SA-3.0-migrated
- Bryce Canyon Sunrise, by Christian Mehlführer, CC-BY-2.5
- Hiking in Bryce, by Eric Henze, Copyright Gone Beyond Guides

Grand Staircase-Escalante National Monument

- Wahweap Hoodoo, by John Fowler, CC-BY-2.0
- Lower calf falls, by Nikater, CC-BY-SA-3.0-migrated
- Devils Garden at Night, by John Fowler, CC-BY-2.0
- In Coyote Gulch, by Kerkphil, CC-BY-SA-3.0
- Little Death Hollow, by Greg Willis, CC-BY-2.0
- Cottonwood Canyon Road, by Umberto Salvagnin, CC-BY-2.0
- Paria Rimrocks, by daveynin, CC-BY-2.0
- Harris Wash, by Greg Willis, CC-BY-2.0

FIND YOUR PARK

In Celebration of a Birthday

In 2016, the National Park Service will turn 100 years old. The national parks have always held a very special place in my heart. They represent some of the best of the best in terms of the natural wonders that America holds. I like the robustness that a national park offers, being fully wilderness in so many different ways, the architectural and historical significance of its buildings, and the educational aspects that the rangers play; including the junior ranger and other programs. Each park protects something that is unique to the world, continually inspiring poets, painters, and patrons every single day. They bring that amazement to all that visit them and connect in a way that we should experience more often.

There was an ask of the national park system to share something and bring a gift to this grandest of birthday celebrations. These books are my gift. Happy birthday NPS, for me you represent America at its best! Here's hoping we can continue to enjoy and protect these lands as a nation for many centuries to come.

The Grand Circle Series Project

This series of hiking guides started from a passion for the area itself. I started visiting the Grand Circle while still in diapers, coming along with my dad on fishing trips up Oak Creek Canyon in the 60's. I have lived within the Grand Circle for much of my life and have hiked many of these places multiple times and through all seasons. I have explored this land for over three decades and each time I went out on a trail or off trail; it was with the same childlike wonder. If a person can fall in love with a place, that is me. Each time I went out, I wanted to share the experience. This sharing started with my friends and then my family, but still, I continued to want to share. Therefore, in that spirit of sharing, I decided to write about my experiences.

The project started by writing my first book on the area, called *A Family Guide to the Grand Circle National Parks*. This travel guide describes a vacation around seven national parks, Zion, Bryce Canyon, Capitol Reef, Canyonlands, Arches, Mesa Verde, and the Grand Canyon. I had fun with the book. I worked with the rangers on the park descriptions and even wrote semi fictional stories to go along with each park. It was great fun sharing the Grand Circle with others.

Describing the national parks along the "main route" was awesome, but I had this larger idea. What if I described every park within the Grand Circle? I had no idea how large such a project would be or how long it would take. I simply started by writing about every park I knew of and then followed up with firsthand accounts for the ones that I hadn't. I received multiple accounts for each trail. Where I had hiked, I wrote my account, researching, and fact checking along the way. Where I hadn't hiked, I worked with others who had, incorporating firsthand accounts from a strong and amazing network of hiking experts and other folks passionate about the area. A tremendous amount of fact checking and support went into this work because while it is nearly impossible for one person to have hiked every trail in this book, I wanted to make sure every trail was described accurately and robustly.

The intent of this work is simple. The Grand Circle Series attempts at gathering every trail for every national park, national monument, national historic park, national recreation area, tribal park, and state park within the Grand Circle. I am certain that there are trails and possibly even parks yet that need to be included. The Browns Canyon National Monument is a great case in point. It was just recently added to the national park system in 2015. That said, after describing nearly 500 trails and after crossing the 100,000-word mark, I realized I was at a stopping point. (This was my 'Forest Gump at Monument Valley' moment).

When it was all done I had described 12 national parks, 31 national monuments, including national historic sites and preserves, 3 national recreation areas, 29 state parks and 4 tribal parks. These 79 parks in all cover 480 hikes and the truth is there are still hikes left to be defined, especially in the larger and more remote parks. I left out unofficial hikes within parks and also left out secret areas only known to locals, as I believe some land is so special that it should be preserved, that if it wants you to visit it, it will call you, it needs no introduction.

So what to do with all these trail descriptions? The intent originally was to put everything into one book, but then I realized that wouldn't be very useful. It would be too big to fit into a daypack and most folks would not make full use of a book covering such a large area. In the end, I decided to split the content into four guides, one each for Nevada, Utah, Arizona and finally one more collectively covering Colorado and New Mexico. These four kept everything to a manageable area of interest.

Each book spills over in its surrounding states just a bit, because that's how I would use such a book. This way if you are planning to hike Black Canyon of the Gunnison National Park using the Colorado/New Mexico trail guide, you can read on to the chapter that describes Canyonlands National Park in nearby Utah, because it's just as amazing, but in a completely different way. For the one person who buys all four books, first off, thank you! Secondly, hopefully you understand why you have four copies of the Four Corners Monument chapter.

I am always looking for feedback on improving these books and for any accuracy, misspellings, gripes, wants, and of course kudos. Please send to gonebeyondguides@gmail.com. I write, design, and publish these works myself.

Happy hiking!

Acknowledgments

First off, I want to thank MRoy Cartography for their wonderful map making, headed by Molly Roy. I came in with a request to make these the best maps out there and she fully delivered.

I am extremely thankful for the constant ebb and flow of feedback from my growing focus group, whom I used day in and day out as a sounding board for ideas, research, and pretty much for every aspect of this book. This is never a one-man shop; I couldn't do what I do without them. These include Ernie, Chris, Frank, Joel, George, Geoff, Jeff, Peggy, John, and Angela.

A special thanks to the National Park Service and its employees. There has never been a time when you weren't able to support this effort, which is remarkable given how much you all do. I truly appreciate all that you do for us as a nation and for all the help and assistance you have given me. To NPS - - Happy 100th birthday!

I also want to thank the states of Utah, Arizona, New Mexico, Colorado, and Nevada. Each of you protects some of the best and most remote lands in the United States. Each state, I commend you for your efforts here.

To my wife Angela and two boys, Everest and Bryce, thank you. The time you have given me to create these books is a true blessing, both in the adventures we have taken and in the many hours writing and editing away you have given me.

You can reach the author through our FaceBook page:

www.facebook.com/GBG.GoneBeyondGuides

ISBN-10:   0-9971370-4-5

ISBN-13:   978-0-9971370-4-0

Eric Henze began his writing career at the age of twelve with a sci fi short titled "5:15", tackling a plot around a timepiece that could end the world. His passion for hiking started in Sedona, Arizona where he lived in his youth. It expanded to peak bagging in the Sierra Nevada Mountains and then the Andes of South America, where he lived as a Peace Corp volunteer for two years, climbing many of the peaks of Ecuador and Peru. A highlight was climbing Sangay, an active volcano that often shoots VW size rocks at climbers to maintain their attention. In his own words, "It was a delight".

His passions for writing, hiking, and adventure have led to a series of guidebooks for both the National Park Service and the California State Parks. A portion of the proceeds of all of his books will go towards directly supporting these parks.

By day, the intrepid author works for a Fortune 50 company helping large enterprises navigate towards, within and beyond the digital revolution. He is lives his family, two awesome boys, a lovely wife, and a blue-eyed merle named Sedona.

His children have noted that his last words will be while driving through the Southwest and seeing some point of interest. Those last words will be, "I'll be right back, I'm going go check that out".

Also Available Within the Grand Circle Series

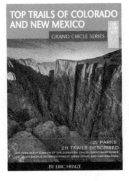

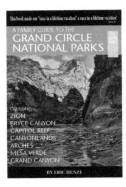

Top Trails of Utah

Top Trails of Arizona

Top Trails of Colorado and New Mexico

A Family Guide to the Grand Circle National Parks

Follow us on Facebook and Twitter!

     facebook.com/GBG.GoneBeyondGuides

     twitter.com/GoneBeyondGuide

All titles published by Gone Beyond Guides